MW01503322

The
Oxford
Dictionary of
American English
workbook

UNIVERSITY PRESS

Contents

These worksheets have been specially designed to help you get to know your dictionary and to use it with ease. As you work your way through Part One, you will learn the dictionary skills that enable you to find what you want quickly and easily. Part Two goes a step further and shows you how your dictionary can help you to increase your vocabulary and use your dictionary for topic based activities.

All of the exercises in this workbook can be done in class or for self-study – either way, they provide an interesting and fun introduction to the **Oxford Dictionary of American English**.

PART ONE
Getting to know your dictionary

1 Introducing the *Oxford Dictionary of American English*

The Oxford Dictionary of American English is a monolingual dictionary that has been written especially for learners of English. The difference between monolingual and bilingual dictionaries is that a *bilingual* dictionary (e.g., Spanish–English) tells you how to translate a word into another language, and a *monolingual* dictionary explains the words in English and helps you to learn how to use them correctly.

This workbook will show you the ways in which the **Oxford Dictionary of American English** can help you in your learning. You will find out how many different kinds of information are found in your dictionary, and you will practice using them so that you become a quick and efficient dictionary user.

A Why use a monolingual dictionary?

Dictionaries are useful for many reasons. The list below shows the 4 most common uses. Number them from 1 to 4 with 1 being the most common. Then compare your list with a partner.

_____ To find the correct spelling of a word.

_____ To find the meaning of a word.

_____ To find the pronunciation of a word.

_____ To find the appropriate use of a word.

> ❶ A learner's dictionary has many uses from explaining the meanings of words to helping you improve your English generally. However, to make the most of your dictionary you have to know how to use it well.

B Looking at an entry

1 Read through the dictionary entries below.

> **dip·lo·mat·ic** /ˌdɪpləˈmætɪk/ *adj.* **1** connected with DIPLOMACY (1): *Diplomatic relations between the two countries have been restored.* **2** clever at dealing with people: *He searched for a diplomatic reply so as not to offend her.* ► **dip·lo·mat·i·cal·ly** /-kli/ *adv.*
>
> **dire** /ˈdaɪər/ *adj.* (*formal*) very bad or serious; terrible: *dire consequences* ◇ *dire poverty*
>
> ►**di·rect¹** /dəˈrɛkt; daɪ-/ *adj.* **1** going from one place to another without turning or stopping; straight: *The most direct route is through the center of town.* ◇ *a direct flight to Hong Kong* **2** with nobody/nothing in between; not involving anybody/anything else: *The President is in direct contact with his Cabinet.* ◇ *Keep the plant away from direct sunlight.* **3** saying what you mean; clear: *Politicians never give a direct answer to a direct question.* [OPP] The opposite for senses 1, 2 and 3 is **indirect 4** (only *before* a noun) complete; exact: *What she did was in direct opposition to my orders.*

a To identify the different parts of the entries, do the following:

1 **Diplomatic** is a headword. Circle the other headwords.

2 What is the number of the headword **direct**? _____

3 Why does it have this number? _____

4 Underline the pronunciation guides.

5 Put a box around the grammatical information.

6 A derivative is a word that is made from the headword and an ending. What derivative is given of **diplomatic**? _____

7 How many meanings are given for **diplomatic**? _____

8 How many examples are given for **dire**? _____

b Now look at the entries **pump¹ – pumpkin** and choose the correct answers to complete these sentences.

1 **Pump** can be a noun or a **verb/preposition/pronoun**.

2 The idiom that means "to do exercises with heavy weights" is **pump steel/pump iron/pump air**.

3 If you fill something with air, you pump it **in/on/up**.

4 There are pictures of pumps at the entries for **car/bus/bicycle** and **shoe/boot/heel**.

5 There is more information about pumpkins in a **picture/note** at **Halloween**.

> **pump¹** /pʌmp/ *noun* [C] **1** a machine that is used for forcing a gas or liquid in a particular direction: *Do you have a bicycle pump? My tire's flat.* ◇ *a gasoline pump* ➋ picture at **bicycle**. **2** a type of formal shoe for women, usually with a high heel ➋ picture at **shoe**.
>
> **pump²** /pʌmp/ *verb* [I,T] to force a gas or liquid to go in a particular direction: *Your heart pumps blood around your body.*
> [IDM] **pump iron** (*informal*) to do exercises in which you lift heavy weights in order to make your muscles stronger
> [PHRV] **pump sth up 1** to fill sth with air, e.g. by using a PUMP¹(1): *to pump up a car tire* **2** to increase the amount, value or volume of sth: *to pump up the loudspeakers*
>
> **pum·per·nick·el** /ˈpʌmpərˌnɪkl/ *noun* [U] a type of heavy dark brown bread made from rye, originally from Germany
>
> **pump·kin** /ˈpʌmpkɪn/ *noun* [C,U] a very large round fruit with thick orange-colored skin that is cooked and eaten like a vegetable: *pumpkin pie* ➋ picture on study page A28-29. ➋ Look also at **jack-o'-lantern** and at the note at **Halloween**.

C The information in the dictionary

Look at this page from the **Oxford Dictionary of American English** and find which types of information help you with the four uses of the dictionary you discussed in A. Does the dictionary give you any other kind of help?

❶ To find out more about the information in the *Oxford Dictionary of American English*, look at the Guide to the dictionary on pp. iv – vii.

Explanations to help you understand in what context a word is used

389   **lift → like**

Headwords. Stars indicate important vocabulary.

Pronunciation

Illustrations help you to understand meanings and build up your vocabulary by learning groups of related words.

Notes help you to learn more about how to use the words correctly or to increase your vocabulary by learning related expressions.

Idioms – fixed expressions with special meanings

Meanings – the different meanings are clearly separated by numbers. Entries for words which have a large number of meanings have **SHORTCUTS** to help you find the right definition quickly.

PHR V **lift off** (used about a rocket or spacecraft) to rise straight up from the ground

★ **lift²** /lɪft/ *noun* **1** [sing.] a feeling of happiness or excitement: *Her words of encouragement gave the whole team a lift.* **2** [C] a free ride in a car, etc.: *Can you give me a lift to the store?* **3** [sing.] an act of lifting or being lifted

lift·off /'lɪftɔf/ *noun* [C] the start of the flight of a rocket or spacecraft: *Only ten seconds to liftoff!*

lig·a·ment /'lɪgəmənt/ *noun* [C] a strong band in a person's or animal's body that holds the bones, etc. together

lights

light bulb   ceiling light   lampshade

battery   flashlight   table lamp   spotlight

★ **light¹** /laɪt/ *noun*
▸ FROM SUN/LAMPS **1** [U] the brightness that allows you to see things: *the light of the sun* ◇ *The light was too bad for us to read by.*

NOTE You may see things by **sunlight, moonlight, firelight, candlelight, lamplight,** etc.

2 [C] something that produces LIGHT (1), e.g. a lamp: *the lights of the city in the distance* ◇ *a neon light* ◇ *That car's lights aren't on.*

NOTE A light can be **on** or **off**: *Why are all the lights on?* You **turn** or **switch** a light **on, off** or **out**: *Should I turn the light on? It's getting dark in here.* ◇ *Please switch the lights off before you leave.*

▸ FOR TRAFFIC **3** [C] one of three colored lights, or a set of these lights (red, yellow and green) that control traffic: *Slow down – there's a red light ahead.*

▸ FOR CIGARETTE **4** [C] something, e.g. a match, that can be used to light a cigarette, start a fire, etc.: *Can you give me a light?*

IDM **come to light** to be found or become known
give sb/get the green light → GREEN¹
in a good, bad, etc. light (used about the way that sth is seen or described by other people) well, badly, etc.: *The newspapers often portray his behavior in a bad light.*
in the light of because of; considering: *We might have to change our decision in the light of what you just said.*
set light to sth to cause sth to start burning
shed light on sth → SHED

★ **light²** /laɪt/ *adj.*
▸ NOT DARK **1** having a lot of LIGHT¹ (1); not dark: *In the summer it's still light at 9 o'clock.* ◇ *a light room*
▸ OF A COLOR **2** (used about a color) pale; not dark: *a light blue sweater*
▸ NOT HEAVY **3** not of great weight; not heavy: *Carry this bag – it's the lightest.* ◇ *I've lost weight – I'm five pounds lighter than I used to be.* ◇ *light clothes* (= for summer)
▸ NOT GREAT **4** not great in amount, degree, etc.:

Traffic downtown is light on Sundays. ◇ *a light prison sentence* ◇ *a light wind* ◇ *a light breakfast*
▸ GENTLE **5** not using much force; gentle: *a light touch on the shoulder*
▸ OF WORK, ETC. **6** (used about work, etc.) easy to do: *light exercise*
▸ NOT SERIOUS **7** not very serious or hard to understand: *light reading*
▸ OF SLEEP **8** not deep: *I've always been a light sleeper.*
▸ OF FOOD/DRINKS **9** (*informal*) (*also* **lite**) (used especially on food packages, in restaurants, etc.) containing less fat, alcohol, or other unhealthy substances that can make people gain weight: *light cheesecake*
▸ **light·ness** *noun* [U]

★ **light³** /laɪt/ *verb* (*pt, pp* **lit** or **light·ed**) **1** [I,T] to begin to burn or to make sth do this: *This match won't light.* ◇ *to light a fire*

NOTE **Lighted** is usually used as an adjective before the noun. **Lit** is used as the past participle of the verb: *Candles were lit in memory of the dead.* ◇ *The church was full of lighted candles.*

2 [T] to give light to sth: *The room was lit with one 40-watt bulb.*

PHR V **light up** (used about sb's face, eyes, etc.) to become bright with happiness or excitement

light⁴ /laɪt/ *adv.* **1** without much luggage: *to travel light* **2** without a lot of fat or oil: *to cook/eat light*

light bulb (*also* **bulb**) *noun* [C] the glass part of an electric lamp that gives out light: *a 60-watt light bulb*

light·en /'laɪtn/ *verb* [I,T] **1** to become lighter in weight or to make sth lighter: *to lighten a load* **2** to become brighter or to make sth brighter

light·er /'laɪt̬ər/ *noun* [C] an object which produces a small flame for lighting cigarettes, etc.

light·heart·ed /'laɪt,hɑrt̬əd/ *adj.* **1** without problems; happy **2** funny; amusing

light·house /'laɪthaʊs/ *noun* [C] a tall building with a light at the top that guides ships or warns them of dangerous rocks, etc.

light·ing /'laɪt̬ɪŋ/ *noun* [U] the quality or type of lights used in a room, building, etc.: *Soft lighting helps to make people more relaxed.*

★ **light·ly** /'laɪtli/ *adv.* **1** in a LIGHT² (5) way: *He touched her lightly on the arm.* **2** not seriously; without serious thought: *We should not take her remarks lightly – this is an important matter.*

light·ning /'laɪtnɪŋ/ *noun* [U] a bright flash of light that appears in the sky during a thunderstorm: *The tree was struck by lightning.*

light·weight /'laɪtweɪt/ *noun* [C], *adj.* **1** (a boxer) weighing between 126 and 135 pounds **2** (a person or thing) weighing less than usual: *a lightweight suit for the summer*

lik·a·ble (*also* **like·a·ble**) /'laɪkəbl/ *adj.* (used about a person) easy to like; pleasant

★ **like¹** /laɪk/ *verb* (not in the continuous tenses) **1** [T] to find sb/sth pleasant; to be fond of sb/sth: *He's nice. I like him a lot.* ◇ *Do you like their new house?* ◇ *I like my coffee with milk.* ◇ *I like playing tennis./*

Examples (in *italics*) show you typical sentences and phrases in which the word is used

Information about the **level of formality** of a word – is it appropriate for written, spoken, informal or formal language?

Phrasal verbs – verbs used with particles in special meanings.

Pronunciation of compound headwords. Multi–word expressions are marked to show you which part carries the emphasis when you say it.

Grammar information shows you how to use a word correctly.

tʃ chin | dʒ June | v van | θ thin | ð then | s so | z zoo | ʃ she

D Understanding short forms and abbreviations

Every dictionary uses short forms and abbreviations in entries to save space. If you know what these abbreviations and short forms mean when you look up a word, it will make using the dictionary much easier.

Look at pages 270–271 of your **Oxford Dictionary of American English** and, with the help of the list of *short forms and symbols* inside the front cover, complete this crossword puzzle.

ACROSS

1 **Fortified** is the _____ participle of **fortify**. (4)

4 _____ is the abbreviation for "idiom". (3)

7 **Frame** is a(n) _____ verb. (10)

10 **Unfortunate** is the _____ of **fortunate**. (8)

12 When **fortune** means "luck" as in *Fortune was not on our side that day*, it is a(n) _____ noun. (11)

13 **Fractionally** is a(n) _____. (6)

15 The third person singular _____ of **fortify** is **fortifies**. (7)

17 The grammar information for **the Fourth of July** tells us that it is a(n) _____ noun. (8)

DOWN

1 **Foul sth up** is a _____ verb. (7)

2 **Forthright** is a(n) _____. (9)

3 The shaded boxes at **foster** and **fox** contain _____. (5)

5 The abbreviation for 'etcetera' is _____. (3)

6 **4WD** is the _____ of **four–wheel drive**. (12)

8 **Fossil** is a(n) _____ noun. (9)

9 **Foundries** is the _____ of **foundry**. (6)

11 The present participle of **fortify** is _____. (10)

14 **Forsook** is the past _____ of **forsake**. (5)

16 Look at the note at **forward**[1]. It gives a list of examples of verbs. The short form used before examples is _____. (2)

2 Finding words quickly

A Alphabetical order using initial letters

The position of a word in a dictionary depends on its first or *initial* letter. Words that begin with the first letters of the alphabet, e.g., *able, begin, cat,* and *dog,* are at the beginning of the dictionary, and words that begin with the last letters of the alphabet, e.g., *visit, what, you,* and *zoo,* are at the end. This is because the words are in **alphabetical order.**

1 a Put each group of words into alphabetical order:

hickory   cedar   yew   magnolia   beech   fir

_____

palmtop   freeware   spellchecker   blog   Webmaster

_____

b Now find the words in your dictionary.
What can you say about each group?

2 a What is the initial of your first name?

_____

b If you are in a class, stand up in groups of eight to ten students, and line up facing the board in alphabetical order by the initial of your first name. If there is more than one student with the same initial, stand next to one another.

c Now compete with the other groups in your class to see who can line up the fastest by the initials of your last names.

d Join together with the other groups and rearrange yourselves by the initials of your last names.

3 a Rearrange the words in the jumbled sentences below into alphabetical order by the first letter of each word to make sentences. Then rearrange these sentences into alphabetical order by the first words of each sentence to make a story. The first sentence has been done for you.

room darkness his enveloped
Darkness enveloped his room.

she'd he show up hoped

_____

wind flickered the candles in

_____

yet returned Betsy hadn't

_____

sleep couldn't well very Alex

_____

b Look up any words you do not know in the dictionary.

c Now complete the story in your own words. You do not need to use alphabetical order. Work together with a partner, if possible.

suddenly, _____

_____

_____

_____

_____

_____

B Alphabetical order with words starting with the same first letter

When words begin with the same letter, the first letter which is different determines the order of the words. For example:

— **paint** appears before **point**
— **point** appears before **police**
— **police** appears before **policy**

Look at the words below. Use the first different letter (the third, fourth, fifth, or sixth) to put the words in alphabetical order. Write a number next to each word.

_1_ line	_____ literature	_____ lining
_____ link	_____ liquid	_____ liqueur
_____ listen	_____ list	_____ lion
_____ lip	_____ literate	_____ liner

C Using Guide Words

In the dictionary, you can see at the top of the page the first and last words which appear on that page. These are called **guide words**. If the word you are looking for comes between these two words alphabetically, it can be found on that page.

1 a Below is a list of jumbled guide words. Put the guide words into pairs by drawing arrows to show which ones go together. (Hint: Use alphabetical order.)

girlfriend	finish	freshen	function
find	getaway	front	godfather
furnished	frisk	good	fuel

b Write a pair of guide words next to each number below in alphabetical order. The first one has been done for you.

1 _find → finish_   4 _____ →

_____   _____
_____   _____
_____   _____

2 _____ →   5 _____ →

_____   _____
_____   _____
_____   _____

3 _____ →   6 _____ →

_____   _____
_____   _____
_____   _____

2 a ⏱ Timed Activity

See how long it takes you to put the following list of words in alphabetical order under the correct pair of guide words from exercise **1**. When you are finished, write down your time here.

_____

goggles	funky	gone
furious	fudge	friction
gofer	frustration	gingerbread
finding	ghost	frighten
funny	finely	fingertip
fine	gingham	fry
fungus	fruitful	gold
friendly	frilly	giraffe

b Check your answers in the dictionary. Take time to check the meanings of any words you do not know.

3 If you are in a class, find a partner and look in the dictionary together to choose two pairs of guide words on pages facing each other. Write a quiz like the one above for another pair of students. Give them the guide words in the wrong order, plus eight words, four from each page, also in the wrong order.

D Finding compound headwords

Some headwords are **compounds**, that is, they are made up of two or
more words. They may be spelled with a hyphen, such as **absent-minded**
or **up-to-date**, or without, like **fish stick**. In the **Oxford Dictionary of
American English**, you can find these headwords in alphabetical order as
if they were a single word:

absenteeism	fishing	uptight
absent-minded	fishing rod	up-to-date
absolute	fish stick	up-to-the-minute
	fishy	uptown

Look at these words and number them in the order that you would expect
to find them in in your dictionary:

fire engine	fire alarm	fire extinguisher
fire	firefighter	fire cracker
firearm	fire department	

E Finding abbreviations

In English, long words and expressions are often shortened, and the first letters
of the words used instead of the whole words. Sometimes they are only used in
writing, but other abbreviations are used in speech because they are easier to
say than a long expression. For example, you will often hear people say "RV"
for "recreational vehicle".

In your **Oxford Dictionary of American English,** you can find abbreviations in
the main part of the dictionary in alphabetical order just like other words:
dizzy, **Dixie**, **DJ**, **DNA**.

Put these words and abbreviations into alphabetical order:
duty-free

dwarf

duty

DVD

Now look up these abbreviations and match them with the subject
area that they relate to:

IPA	science
AI	politics
VP	computers
ISP	health
UPC	shopping
Rx	language learning

F Finding derivatives and inflected forms

If you cannot find the **word** you need in the dictionary, ask yourself:

Is this word a **derivative?** If so, what is the **base form** of this word? A **derivative** is a word that has developed from another word, a **base form**. The **base form** is the form of the word without **prefixes** (e.g. redo) or **suffixes** (e.g. **doable**). (See Section 5 for more on prefixes and suffixes.)

1 Look up these derivatives and write down the headword under which they appear in the dictionary:

presidential _____

prettily _____

protester _____

rapidity _____

realization _____

substitution _____

half-heartedly _____

doubtfully _____

confiscation _____

anorexic _____

The **base form** is also the present tense of a verb (walked) or the singular form of a noun (watches). (Note that irregular verb forms and plurals have their own entries, as do many common derivatives.)

2 Write down the headword that you would look up to find the meanings of these words:

traveled _____

asking _____

waits _____

looking _____

hated _____

stones _____

weighing _____

disks _____

friskier _____

handymen _____

slipping _____

3 Idioms and phrasal verbs

Idioms

An idiom is a particular combination of words which has a special meaning that is difficult to guess, even if you know the meanings of the individual words in it. In order to find an idiom in the **Oxford Dictionary of American English**, you need to choose the first most important word in it (ignoring words like 'to' and 'the'). You will find the idiom in the idioms section, marked **IDM**. If you do not find the meaning there, there will be a cross-reference telling you where to go in the dictionary to find it.

A Match the sentences to the pictures and then fill in the blanks with the parts of the body from the list. You may use each word only once.

head eye ears nose chest head
back mind heart arm heels feet

a ☐ There's something I need to get off my _____ .

b ☐ I don't know what's wrong with the boss today. I only asked a question and she bit my _____ off!

c ☐ We weren't really arguing until Bob came along and decided to stick his _____ in.

d ☐ I can't possibly meet you for lunch today. I'm up to my _____ in work at the moment.

e ☐ As she walked up the aisle towards Gary, Linda started to get cold _____ .

f ☐ When John left me for another woman, he broke my _____ .

g ☐ I sit near the water's edge so I can keep an _____ on Amy.

h ☐ Oh all right, I'll come and watch it with you. You've twisted my _____ .

i ☐ I fell _____ over _____ in love with her.

j ☐ As I walked away, I could hear them whispering about me behind my _____ .

k ☐ He took a long time in the store because he couldn't make up his _____ which T-shirt to buy.

❺

❻

❼

❽

> I'll have the plain one

> No, the striped one.

❾

❿

⓫

❶
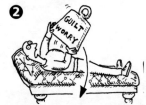

❸

❷

❹

B Replace the word or phrase in **dark type** in sentences 1–10 with one of the idioms from the list below, changing verb forms, pronouns, etc. as necessary.

▶ It *would make me very sad* if anything happened to my cat.

▶ It *would break my heart* if anything happened to my cat.

have/get cold feet	get sth off your chest
twist sb's arm	make up your mind
stick your nose in(to sth)	behind sb's back
be up to your ears in sth	keep an eye on sb/sth
head over heels in love	bite sb's head off
break sb's heart	

1 Could you **watch** my bags for me while I go into the store, please?

2 The way we bring up the children is our business. I don't want your mother **interfering**!

3 Mark and Emma are both still **crazy about each other** even after five years.

4 He was going to report it to the police, but at the last minute he **felt too scared** and decided to keep quiet.

5 Why not tell him how you feel? It might do you good to **talk about it**.

6 Fran says she's too busy to come to the party tonight. See if you can **persuade her**.

7 You'll just have to **decide** which one you want. I'm not waiting any longer!

8 When I asked him what he wanted to eat, he just **shouted at me**.

9 It's not fair of us to discuss Jo's work **without her knowing about it**.

10 We're too busy because we just moved house and we **have lots of** boxes that need unpacking.

C Handy expressions

Find **hand** in your dictionary. There are several other idioms with "hand" in them, but you may have to look up the meanings under another word. For example, the definition of "be an old hand (at sth)" is at **old**.

Find the idiom using "hand" that means:
a be experienced in doing something
b pass from one owner to another
c not under control
d available
e get into a stronger position

Phrasal verbs

Phrasal verbs are two- and three-word phrases made up of verbs and prepositions and/or adverbs. Like an **idiom**, the meaning of a phrasal verb is different than the meaning of the words which make up the **phrasal verb**. (It is important to not **give up** too easily.) (Look at pages A4 and A5 in your dictionary for more on phrasal verbs.)

Phrasal verbs are found within the entry of the first word of the phrase (**give** for "give up") in a section labeled PHR V.

Some particles have a particular meaning that they keep when they are used with various different verbs, for example **back, on** and **off**.

D Look at these sentences

▶ *She wrote to him but he didn't **write back**.*

▶ *I'll loan you the money if you **pay** me **back** next week.*

▶ ***Go on**. I want to know what happens next!*

▶ *They liked the hotel so much that they **stayed on** for an extra week.*

▶ *When I picked up the mug the handle **came off**.*

▶ *I didn't pay the bill and now my phone's been **cut off**.*

Now match the particles on the left with their meanings on the right

back	separate, no longer attached
on	in return
off	continuing

E Fill in the missing particle (**back, on** or **off**) in these sentences:

1 I lent that book to George last week, but he hasn't given it _____ yet.

2 The police have sealed _____ the street where the attack took place.

3 When you've finished with the book please pass it _____ to the next student.

4 Louis got into trouble for talking _____ to the teacher when she told him off in class.

5 Carry _____ with your work. I'll be right back.

6 The road branches _____ to the left a little way up ahead.

Opposites

Often you can find phrasal verbs that have opposite meanings to each other. It may help you to remember them if you learn them together.

F Match up the following sentences into pairs with opposite meanings, then write the pairs in the spaces below.

1 It was getting dark so I **turned on** the light

2 Don't leave your bag on the floor like that – **pick** it **up**!

3 It's cold – **put** your coat **on**.

4 I bought Jon a present to **cheer** him **up**.

5 You should **check in** at reception as soon as you arrive.

6 I **pulled over** to the side of the road to look at the map.

7 I tried to learn the guitar but **gave up** after a few weeks.

8 My dad is coming to **pick** me **up** at ten.

A I can **drop you off** on my way home if you like.

B You have to **check out** of the hotel before noon.

C **Take off** that silly hat!

D I've decided to **take up** aerobics.

E Did you see that? That driver **pulled out** right in front of me.

F Don't forget to **turn off** the TV before you go to bed.

G He **put** the books **down** on the desk.

H Don't let the exams **get** you **down**.

turn sth on   _____

put sth on   _____

check in   _____

give up   _____

pick sth up   _____

cheer sb up   _____

pull over   _____

pick sb up   _____

G Match a verb in the left-hand box with a preposition from the right-hand box. Check your answers in your dictionary.

add	up
plug	down
weigh	up
perk	in

Now look at the pictures below and fill in the blanks in the sentences. Don't forget to use the correct form of the verb in each sentence.

a Tom _____ _____ when he heard he had won.

b After dinner he _____ _____ the check.

c Bill was _____ _____ with luggage.

d You have to _____ _____ the speakers here.

For more information about phrasal verbs, look at study page A4 in your **Oxford Dictionary of American English**.

4 Finding the right meaning

A Definitions

The explanations of the meanings of words in your **Oxford Dictionary of American English** are written in clear, simple language to help you to understand new vocabulary.

Here are some of the words that you will often find in definitions:

person	event	vehicle
material	practice	sport
substance	machine	dish

1 Now try to match the vocabulary items below with one of the categories above. If you are not sure, look them up in your dictionary.

bake sale	Botox	cold-calling
enchilada	paragliding	personal trainer
snowblower	snowmobile	spandex

It is useful to be able to describe something when you don't know the word for it, or to be able to explain the meaning of a word to somebody else. You can do this in general terms, for example,

▶ *It's a type of …*
▶ *It's someone/a person who …*
▶ *It's a way of …ing*
▶ *It's a place where …*

2 Look up the words in the list below and write down one or two words from each definition to help you remember the meaning. Then, with a partner, ask each other questions and try to give a general answer:

▶ STUDENT A: *What's pesto?*
   STUDENT B: *It's a type of sauce.*
      What's a petting zoo?

pesto	feng shui	fanzine
Webmaster	palmtop	smoothie
petting zoo	shiitake	self-starter
rafting		

3 Each of the following definitions contains one of the words mentioned in Section A. See if you can match them with the words in the box below.

a _____ a soft gray **material** which does not burn and which was often used in the past to protect against heat. It can cause serious diseases if you breathe it in.

b _____ a **person** who lives by asking people for money, food, etc. on the streets

c _____ the sweet sticky yellow **substance** that is made by bees and that people eat

d _____ a **machine** in a building that is used for carrying people or goods from one floor to another

e _____ an **event** or a situation that causes great sadness

f _____ a **sport** in which two people fight and try to throw each other to the floor

g _____ a large **vehicle** in which you can sleep, cook, etc. and that you can drive around while you are on vacation, or a similar vehicle that can be pulled by a car or small truck

h _____ an Indonesian and Malaysian **dish** consisting of small pieces of meat or fish cooked on sticks and served with a sauce made with peanuts

i _____ the **practice** of doing experiments on live animals for medical or scientific research

satay	asbestos	vivisection
beggar	elevator	camper
tragedy	wrestling	honey

B Call my bluff

Look up **bluff** and read entry 1 to make sure you know what it means. Now you are going to play a game called "Call My Bluff." In this game you will practice the skill of bluffing.

a If you are in a class, work in pairs. Alternatively, find a friend to play with.

b Choose a word in the dictionary you think your friend, or another pair, does not know.

c Make up a definition for the word of your own.

d Tell your friend, or the other pair, two definitions of the word: your made up definition, and the real definition from the dictionary.

e Ask your friend, or the other pair, to try to guess which definition is real.

f Switch roles. Listen to your friend's or the other pair's definitions and try to guess which one is the real one.

The person or pair who guesses the most right answers is the winner!

C Choosing the right meaning

Many English words have more than one meaning, and in the dictionary you will find entries that have several definitions, each with a number in front of it. You will also find that there is sometimes more than one entry for a spelling.

Look up the words for the parts of the body in the picture below. Scan the different entries and definitions to find the one which matches one of the meanings below. Fill in the table with the name of the body part, the number of the definition, and the number of the entry where relevant.

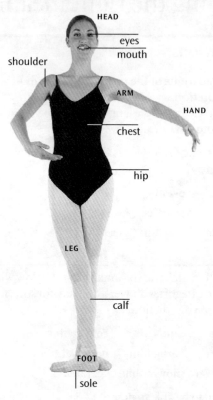

	Body Part	Entry number	Definition number
1 a container, usually with a lid that is fastened on one side			
2 to be in charge of or to lead something			
3 the place where a river enters the ocean			
4 12 inches			
5 a small flat sea fish			
6 very fashionable	*hip*		
7 to prepare yourself to fight			
8 a young cow			
9 to give or pass something to somebody			
10 one part or section of a trip, competition, etc.			
11 the part at one end of a needle that the thread passes through			
12 to accept responsibility for something			

D Using context

When a word has more than one meaning and each meaning has its own definition, grammar and examples in the dictionary, how will you know which one to choose? In the **Oxford Dictionary of American English** the first definition is the most common one, but the meaning you are looking for may be one of the less common ones. To be sure that you have found the right one, you will always have to think about the *context* of the word, that is, the other words around it and the subject matter of what you are reading, writing or talking about.

It may also help you to look at other parts of the entry for more information relating to each meaning:

- examples (in *italics*)
- notes (within parentheses) which apply to individual definitions
- grammar information
- illustrations
- grammar or usage notes (in shaded boxes)

1 Read this sentence:

▶ *I prefer lean meat – I don't like fat.*

and then look up **lean** in your dictionary.

a How many entries are there for lean?

_____

b What parts of speech are they? _____

c Is **lean** in the example sentence above an adjective or a verb? _____

d Which of the meanings in that entry is the one you need? _____

e What helps you to find it? _____

Now look at this sentence:

▶ *He leaned his ladder against the wall.*

f What part of speech is **lean** here?

_____

g Is it meaning 1, 2 or 3? _____

h Which piece of grammar information tells you this? _____

> ❶ Remember, in the **Oxford Dictionary of American English** the first definition is the most common use.

When a word has a large number of different meanings, this dictionary helps you to find the right one quickly using SHORTCUTS.

Look at the entry for wing:

> ★ **wing**¹ /wɪŋ/ *noun*
> ▸ OF BIRD/INSECT **1** [C] one of the body parts that a bird, an insect, etc. uses for flying
> ▸ OF PLANE **2** [C] one of the two long parts that stick out from the side of an airplane and support it in the air
> ▸ OF BUILDING **3** [C] a part of a building that sticks out from the main part or that was added on to the main part: *the maternity wing of the hospital*
> ▸ OF POLITICAL PARTY **4** [C, usually sing.] a group of people in a political party that have particular beliefs or opinions: *the right wing of the Republican party* ➲ Look at **left-wing** and **right-wing**.
> ▸ IN THEATER **5 the wings** [pl.] (in a theater) the area at the sides of the stage where you cannot be seen by the audience

It has five different meanings, but the words in CAPITALS at the beginning of each section give you an idea very quickly of where you could look first, because you will already know what the text you are reading or the idea you are thinking of is about.

If you read the sentence *The bird had an injured wing*, you can see straight away that this is referring to the first meaning of **wing**, but if the text you are reading is about politics, the meaning you want is likely to be number 4. If someone says '*My room is in the North Wing*' he or she must be talking about a building, so you need to look at number 3, but if you find a sentence like '*The actors waited nervously in the wings*', you should look at meaning 5 which has to do with the theater.

2 Find the entry for **service**¹ and use the SHORTCUTS there to decide quickly which meaning you would look up to help you understand these sentences:

a Major Smith joined the service at the age of 19.
b On Sundays they attended services at the local church.
c She was presented with an award after twenty years of service to the company.
d Roddick hit a great service and won the game.
e The service at the Blue Seas Restaurant was excellent.
f A gift-wrapping service is now available.

Now do the same for **strong**¹.

g Our neighbors have very strong feelings about the building of the new highway. ___
h I can't use this cheese. It is too strong for this recipe. ___
i Working on the construction site has made him very strong. ___
j Those shopping bags aren't as strong as they used to be. They keep breaking. ___
k John's computer skills make him the strongest applicant for the position. ___

5 Word families

Word families are groups of words which are all related to one base word. In Section 2, you saw how words are made up of base words and additions such as beginnings or endings. Understanding the meaning of the base words and how they can be altered will help you to understand new words faster, and help you to build your vocabulary.

A Knowing the part of speech

The different members of a word family can have different parts of speech, e.g., noun, verb, adjective, adverb, etc. Knowing a word's part of speech will help you to understand both its meaning and usage.

1 Match one definition and one example to each part of speech below. To check your answers, look up the words in **dark type** in the dictionary.

noun
Definition _____
Example _____

verb
Definition _____
Example _____

adjective
Definition _____
Example _____

adverb
Definition _____
Example _____

Definitions
- a word or group of words that is used to indicate an action or state
- a word used with a noun that tells you more about it
- a word that adds information to a verb, adjective, phrase, or adverb
- a word that is the name of a person, place, thing, or idea

Examples
▶ *The cat and dog glared at each other **angrily**.*
▶ *We **are** students.*
▶ *All the **best** students got above 90% on the test.*
▶ *Those **words** are hard to understand.*

2 Scan your **Oxford Dictionary of American English** to find an example of each of the following:

a noun _____

b verb _____

c adjective _____

d adverb _____

Many words can be used as more than one part of speech. When you are looking up a word, you will know which part of speech you want by its **context** (= the words before and after it).

3 Look up the following words and fill in the table by:

a putting a check (✔) in the box for the different parts of speech listed for each one

b writing down the entry numbers of the parts of speech which are similar in meaning and those which are different from the others in meaning. The first one has been done for you.

	noun	verb	adjective	adverb	similar in meaning	different in meaning
fake	✔	✔	✔		1, 2, 3	
gaze						
marvel						
inside						
express						
fair						
light						
prompt						
chow						
forward						

There are other parts of speech which you will see listed after the pronunciation guide in an entry, such as **determiner, conjunction, article, interjection, preposition** and **pronoun**. Remember, knowing the function of the word you are looking up in the sentence is always helpful in understanding the meaning of the word itself.

4 Match these words to their part of speech:

against	**determiner**
every	**conjunction**
hey	**article**
him	**interjection**
the	**preposition**
whether	**pronoun**

5 a Decide which part of speech these words are.

• Put a box around the adjectives.

• Put a circle around the adverbs.

• Put a check (✔) on the conjunctions.

1 **global**
2 **irritably**
3 **friendly**
4 **while**
5 **greatly**
6 **whether**
7 **unless**
8 **mainly**
9 **leisurely**
10 **although**
11 **soon**
12 **spontaneous**
13 **wryly**
14 **undisclosed**
15 **or**

b To check your answers, try to find your way around this maze, using your answers to direct you. If you cannot continue through the maze, your answer was incorrect. Look that word or phrase up in the dictionary to correct your mistake.

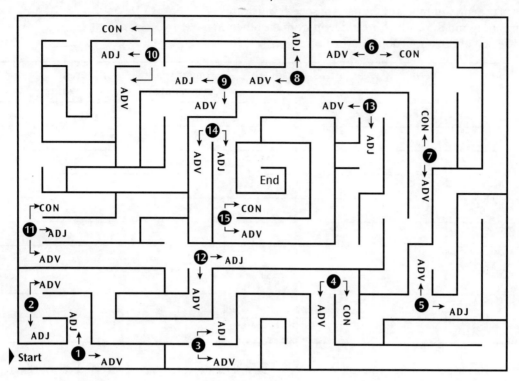

B Prefixes and suffixes

You can change the meaning of a word by adding a prefix (e.g., un-, dis-, ex-, bi-, etc.) to the beginning, and you can change its part of speech by adding a suffix (e.g., -ly, -ness, -able, -ful, etc.) to the end. Knowing what each prefix means, and what each suffix does to a word, will help you to understand many unfamiliar words. You will find information about word formation on Study Pages A6 and A7. There is also a list of prefixes and suffixes on pages 814 and 815 in your dictionary.

1 Look at the study pages A6 and A7, which categorize prefixes or suffixes by meaning and function. List below two prefixes or suffixes for each category.

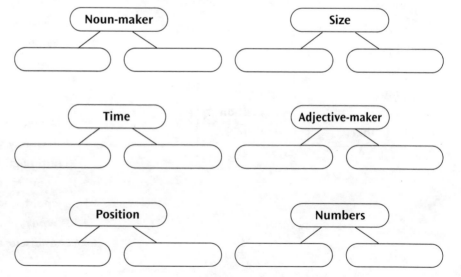

2 **a** All of the prefixes listed in the chart below can be used to change the meaning of certain words to their opposites. Look up the following words in your **Oxford Dictionary of American English** to match the words with the correct prefixes and then write them in the chart.

grateful	polite	obedient	legible
honest	sensitive	rational	adequate
logical	tolerant	pure	responsible

❗ Note that the opposite of each of the words listed appears in the entry for the word. There is also a separate entry for each of the opposites.

im-			
un-	*ungrateful*		
ir-			
in-			
il-			
dis-			

b Write a sentence for each of the words in the box and for their opposites in the chart.

c All of the suffixes listed in the chart below can be added to verbs and nouns to form the word for a person who does something as a job or hobby, or who studies a subject. Look at the entry for each word in the **Oxford Dictionary of American English** to find the correct suffixes and write them in the chart. (Notice that sometimes there is a slight change in the spelling.) Two of the words can be used twice.

direct	act	attend	science
assist	art	create	train
music	account	electric	comedy
employ	teach		

-er			
-or	*director*		
-ist			
-ian			
-ee			
-ant			

3 a All of the words listed below can all be found in this word search puzzle. Each word has either a prefix or suffix attached to it. Be careful – there are also some incorrect prefixes and suffixes in the puzzle!

You can find the words by reading from:

- top to bottom   ↓
- bottom to top   ↑
- left to right   →
- diagonally   ↗

Now write the words below with their correct prefixes or suffixes on the lines below. The first one has been done for you.

success	ordinary	usual	violent
complete	typical	operate	polite
danger	neighbor	caution	delight
comfort			

1   *successfully*

2 _____

3 _____

4 _____

5 _____

6 _____

7 _____

8 _____

9 _____

10 _____

11 _____

12 _____

13 _____

```
U N P A B L E A N T E S E D I N A U T O N
B I R E D E L I G H T F U L L O N E N T L
D E E C I N I N C O M P L E T E H O D U E
E L T O S D R M I S P O L I T E N E S S R
D B Y M C E R A S H O N O H A N A X U I S
A A P E O R M L L U C K L E S S I R P N S
N N I N M F O I S X C O M A N Y N E W Y E
G O C D F O R S I W U C U T T S Y S E R N
E I A I O R E T F M L N E N O P A I S Q E
R T L T R S T I A U H I E S J K R S T L T
O U L L T L H C F B C L D E S F E T P G A
U A Y E E E A L K A O U I M E F L A O E R
S C H O N I A L Y I S T I C R E U B B L E
P E S T I U N A V T I W I P A U W L D E P
A R F I S H O N W A D I K A L I E E L R O
E P P U N A O D H A L F A M A J U N G Y O
L A N T I N E I G H B O R H O O D H O L C
D U E X T R A O R D I N A R Y N E S S M R
```

b Make sentences with the words that you have found. Remember, the example sentences at the entries in the **Oxford Dictionary of American English** can help you.

C Synonyms and antonyms

Your **Oxford Dictionary of American English** helps you to build your vocabulary by learning related words. For example, when you look up the word **minimize** you see the symbol **OPP** and you find out that the opposite, or antonym, of **minimize** is **maximize**. If you look at the entry for **strong-minded**, you will see another word with a very similar meaning: **determined**. This is shown with the symbol **SYN** .

1 Synonyms

a Read the following article, looking carefully at the words in dark type. For each of these words there is another word in the passage which means the same thing. Underline the synonyms for the words.

It was during a **blackout** caused by a **snowstorm** that Joe Hale's five-year-old daughter Grace got sick. Recognizing that the situation was very **grave**, Joe decided he had to get her to the hospital twenty miles away down in the valley. **Apparently undaunted** by the blizzard, Joe set off in his pickup on his **perilous** journey. It would have been a dangerous trip at any time, but that night the driving snow made it almost impossible to see the edge of the road, and beside it was a steep drop. Joe knew the mountains, however, and at first he was not **perturbed**. "I only became alarmed when I realized I was running out of gas," he remembers. "I knew Grace's condition was very serious and I was **petrified** that we wouldn't make it to the hospital in time." Soon, Joe ran out of gas, and the truck ground to a halt. Undeterred, he wrapped the little girl up in a blanket and continued on foot, carrying her in his arms. It was a seemingly **interminable** trek. "I just kept going," he says, "but I was terrified that the hospital might have been hit by the power outage, too, and there would be endless delays." Fortunately, his fears were unfounded – the hospital generators were working and Grace received immediate treatment, which helped her to make a full recovery. **Self-effacing** as ever, Joe says: "I just did what any father would have done." His daughter thinks he's too modest. "Dad's a real hero," she says. "He saved my life."

b Write the synonyms you found in the passage next to the words.

blackout _____

snowstorm _____

grave _____

apparently _____

undaunted _____

perilous _____

perturbed _____

petrified _____

interminable _____

self-effacing _____

c Now look up the words in the dictionary and check that you have the correct synonyms.

2 Opposites/Antonyms

a Read the following newspaper article:

The plan to build a new road into Northport from the

failure

west is expected to be a **success** according to the mayor's office. If the estimates are **accurate,** it will be **possible** to drive from Sanford to Northport in only 20 minutes. Local business people agree that the **advantage** for them is that this will **increase** the number of people using the mall and the surrounding restaurants, especially on the weekends.

A transportation system will be added, providing a **cheap, comfortable** and **convenient** way into town from Sanford and hopefully solving the problem of limited parking in Northport. The new buses are **efficient** and **suitable** for disabled passengers.

The plan also seems to be **popular** with local people. A survey has shown that at least 70% of the residents **approve** of the idea and feel that it is the most **satisfactory** solution to the area's problems.

b Look up the words in **dark type,** and write their opposites above each word.

c Imagine it is a year since the new road opened and things have not happened the way the people had hoped. There have been many problems such as crowded stores, traffic jams, increased pollution and parking problems. Use these ideas and your list of opposites to write a letter to the mayor's office describing the disadvantages of the plan.

6 Using information about grammar and usage

Understanding the meaning of a word is only part of learning a language. You also need to know how to *use* the word correctly. Your **Oxford Dictionary of American English** provides important grammatical and usage information for each word. This information will help you to use words correctly in the right context, which includes:
- choosing words that are appropriate for the type of language;
- using the words in a way that is grammatically correct.

A **Nouns**

This dictionary answers the following questions about nouns:
- Is the noun **countable** [C] (= can be counted, e.g. *one pen, two pens*), e.g., pencil, pen, and book, or **uncountable** [U] (= cannot be counted, e.g. *some sugar*), e.g., sugar, water, and money?
- Is the noun always **singular** [sing.], e.g. gist, or always **plural** [plural], e.g. belongings.
- Does the countable noun have an **irregular plural form** (*pl.*)?
- Is the noun used with a specific **preposition**?

1 a Look up the following nouns and write the grammatical information that you find in the entry next to each one.

1 **mouse**
   _____

2 **eyeglasses**
   _____

3 **candidacy**
   _____

4 **the Irish**
   _____

5 **knowledge**
   _____

6 **the last⁴**
   _____

7 **restriction**
   _____

b The sentences below use the nouns in Exercise **1** incorrectly. Use the grammar information you noted in **1a** to cross out and correct the mistakes.

1 We got a cat last week to catch all the *mouses* we have in the barn.
   _____

2 I lost my other *eyeglass*, so now I have only this pair.
   _____

3 Five presidential candidates have already announced their *candidacies*.
   _____

4 The *Irish* we met on vacation was a really nice guy.
   _____

5 Children today seem to have more *knowledges* about the world than they used to.
   _____

6 Jenny, Michele, and Lee were *the lasts* to finish the exam.
   _____

7 There is a new *restriction* in the exportation of meat.
   _____

c Check your corrections in the dictionary.

B Verbs

The **Oxford Dictionary of American English** answers the following questions about verbs:

- Is the verb **transitive** [T] (= has an object), e.g., "We *put it* there," or **intransitive** [I] (= has no object), e.g., "We *arrived*," or **both** [IT], e.g., "Please help," and "Please help me?"
- Is the verb **irregular** in the way it forms the **past tense** (*pt*) and/or **past participle** (*pp*), e.g., *sing - sang - sung, teach - taught - taught, choose - chose - chosen*, etc.?
- Is the verb **irregular** in the way it forms the **3rd person singular in the present**, e.g., *do - does*?
- Is there a verb **tense** or **form** in which it more often appears, e.g. *hospitalize is usually used in the passive*?
- Is there a **preposition** it is normally used with, e.g. *agree with* somebody?
- Does the final letter of the verb get doubled when forming the present or past participle or past tense, e.g., *bat - ba<u>tt</u>ing, ba<u>tt</u>ed*?
- If the verb is a transitive phrasal verb, is it **inseparable**, e.g., "No one can *do without* water," or **separable**, e.g., "Don't forget to *turn* the lights *off*?"

1 a Look up the following verbs and write the grammar information that you find in the entry next to each one.

1 disturb _____

2 qualify _____

3 ban _____

4 subsist _____

5 acquaint _____

6 undo _____

7 look up _____

b The sentences below use the verbs in Exercise **4** incorrectly. Use the grammar information you noted above to cross out and correct the mistakes.

1 Oh sorry! I didn't mean to *disturb*.

_____

2 She hopes to get a job in computer programming when she *qualifys*.

_____

3 Both athletes may be *baned* from taking part in the Olympics.

_____

4 They *subsist* their families on rice and a few vegetables.

_____

5 She wanted to *acquaint herself* to the area.

_____

6 Sam's mistake *undoed* all his previous efforts at building trust between himself and his employer.

_____

7 If you don't know the word, *look up* it in the dictionary.

_____

c Check your corrections in the dictionary.

C Adjectives

Your **Oxford Dictionary of American English** gives you information about the grammar of adjectives, for example:

- Whether or not an adjective can only be used **before or after a noun**, e.g. *countless, alike*
- How the **comparisons** of the adjective or adverb are formed, e.g. happy - happ*ier* - happ*iest*
- Whether the adjective is used with a specific **preposition**, e.g. *fond of* somebody
- Whether or not the adjective and adverb are the **same word**, e.g. *fast*

1 Look up the following words and (circle) the adjectives which must be used before a noun and <u>underline</u> the adjectives which must be used after a noun.

(outward)   <u>alone</u>   amiss   economic

darned   glad   asleep   capital

2 With most short adjectives, you make the comparative and superlative forms by adding -**er** or -**est**. What is different about these adjectives?

cosy   dry   flat   dim   far   good   bad

Check the entries in your dictionary if you are not sure.

3 Some adjectives are followed by a particular preposition. Look at these sentences and decide which of the prepositions is correct. Then check your answers in your dictionary.

a   He was very ashamed *of/for/with* what he had done.
b   She's incapable *to/of/by* getting anything done quickly!
c   They said I wasn't eligible *for/on/at* a scholarship.
d   I was very dissatisfied *about/of/with* their work.
e   Is this suitable *to/for/at* a student at my level?
f   His point was not relevant *to/about/at* the discussion.
g   It's typical *to/for/of* him to blame somebody else.
h   I'm terrified *on/of/from* rats.

4 Circle the adjectives which have the same form for the adverb.

able	(early)	fast	far	consequent
cool	right	sufficient	extreme	long

5 Look up the following adjectives and adverbs. Scan each entry for sets of parentheses ( ) with information about special uses. Then write the adjective or adverb in the correct box in the table below. Write the definition number where necessary. Words can be used more than once.

deep	delicate	strong	bright
decent	demanding	eccentric	demonstrative
pastel	elastic	shrill	bland
high	hot		

Adjectives and adverbs used to talk about:

people	*decent* ²				
sounds					
colors					
flavors and food					
jobs					
objects, things and materials					

D Grammar and usage notes

Many entries in the **Oxford Dictionary of American English** include shaded notes which provide important additional information. These notes provide one or a combination of the following:

- further information about the meaning of the headword, or one of its derivatives, idioms, or phrasal verbs
- points about grammar or usage
- vocabulary-building notes with related words, synonyms and antonyms
- help in avoiding common mistakes
- further information about how a word is normally used or if it has any special uses.

Using notes to identify errors

1 Your dictionary contains lots of notes which explain words that people often confuse or grammatical points which people often get wrong. In each of the following sentences, there is an error. Try to identify it and then write out the sentence correctly underneath.

a I don't have an own car.

_____

b He came to Chicago to look for a work.

_____

c The police said there were not enough evidences to convict the man.

_____

d You need a permission to park here.

_____

e I don't have enough place for all my books on my shelf.

_____

f She had the possibility to do an exchange with a student in Italy.

_____

g The thieves broke in and robbed the TV and the computer.

_____

h My grandmother can't come to visit me – the long travel would be too tiring for her.

_____

i The family has moved here three years ago.

_____

j It's sure that she'll get a good grade.

_____

k He used to work for our company, but I don't know where he works actually.

_____

l It's a too big job for me to do on my own.

_____

Now look at the notes at the following entries and see if you found the errors:

own	**work**	**evidence**
permission	**place**	**possibility**
rob	**travel**	**ago**
sure	**actually**	**too**

E Formal and informal language

Most words can be used in a variety of situations, whether you are speaking or writing. However, some words are more often used in the *spoken* language and others more in *written* language. Some are only used when the context is *formal*, for example serious books, articles and speeches, and others are common in *informal* situations, such as normal conversation or letters to friends. The least formal category is *slang*, which is used among groups of friends, but is not suitable, for example, for writing in an essay or paper. Slang words are often only used for a short time and then they are replaced by new expressions. Other words also become more or less popular over time. Words that are no longer in common use are labeled *old-fashioned* in the dictionary.

1 In some situations the words that are used are more formal than in normal conversation. Look at the signs, instructions, forms, and speech bubbles below. The language of the signs, instructions, and forms is more formal than in the speech bubbles. Use the dictionary to help you choose the correct verb for each blank. Then fill in the blanks.

1	permit	6	choose
2	select	7	let
3	obtain	8	take off
4	remove	9	leave out
5	omit	10	get

Ⓖ

parking permit from the Visitor's Center

Ⓐ

The college does not ▢ skateboarding in the parking lot.

Ⓓ 'All the cakes look delicious. I don't know which to _____.'

Ⓗ 'I can't do question 4 so I'm going to _____ it _____ .'

Ⓑ

Photocopying

1 _____

number of copies

2 Press green button

Ⓔ If you're too hot, _____ your coat _____ !

Ⓘ 'My mom would never _____ me skip school.'

Ⓒ

7 Are you a full-time student?

Yes No

If "yes" _____ numbers 8 and 9.

8 Name and address of employer

Ⓕ

Cooking Instructions

1 Heat oven to 350°

2 _____ wrapper

3 Place dish in oven

Ⓙ Is there a bookstore near here? I want to _____ that book

2 Informal language

You will hear many words used in conversation that are informal or slang, that is, you would not read them in formal language, such as a serious article in the newspaper. In your **Oxford Dictionary of American English** these words are marked *informal* or *slang*.

Look at the informal and slang words in the box on the left and try to match them up with the neutral words on the right. Then look the words up in your dictionary and see whether you were right.

phat	president
scuzzy	vomit
wacko	mess around
wig out	very bad
upchuck	excellent
wack	dirty and unpleasant
prez	crazy
skanky	in large numbers or amounts
out the wazoo	become very excited
putz around	very unpleasant

7 Pronouncing and spelling words

Pronunciation

Many students find the pronunciation guide in a dictionary hard to use because the phonetic alphabet is difficult to read and remember. The **Oxford Dictionary of American English** makes using the pronunciation guide easy by printing a key to the phonetic symbols at the bottom of the A – Z dictionary pages.

A Reading pronunciation markings and symbols

1 Look at the word **conversation** in the dictionary.

   a Draw the mark which is used to show the syllable breaks in the headword

   _____

> ❗ Note: Information on syllable breaks is in the headword itself. Pronunciation help for each headword follows the headword between slashes / /.

   b How many syllables are there in *conversation*?

   _____

   c The phonetic spelling of **conversation** is written between the slashes. Are the syllables marked there?

   _____

The pronunciation information between the slashes (/ /) shows how to pronounce each letter and which syllables are **stressed** (= said with more force). Note that every word with two syllables or more has at least one stressed syllable. Many words with three or more syllables have two stressed syllables, one with **primary stress** (= said with the most force) and one with **secondary stress** (= said with less force than the syllable with primary stress).

2 Look at **conversation** in the dictionary again.

   a The syllable with primary stress is -*sa*- . Draw the mark which is used to show this.

   _____

   b The first syllable (*con*-) has secondary stress. Draw the mark which is used to show secondary stress.

   _____

3 Look at the phonetic alphabet on the inside of the back cover of the **Oxford Dictionary of American English**.

   a What are the two categories the alphabet is divided into?

   _____

   b How many symbols are there in each category?

   _____

> ❗ Reminder: You do not have to memorize these symbols because they are written at the bottom of each A–Z dictionary page. You will find all the vowels at the bottom of two pages, and the consonants at the bottom of the next two, and so on throughout the dictionary.

B Reading phonetic spelling

1 Look at these examples for the words *phonetic* and *symbol* and see how the phonetic symbols correspond to the spelling.

pho·net·ic /fəˈnɛt̮ɪk/ *adj.* **1** connected with the sounds of human speech **2** using a system for writing a language that has a different sign for each sound: *the phonetic alphabet* ▶ **pho·net·i·cal·ly** /-kli/ *adv.*

ph	o	n	e	t	i	c
f	ə	n	ɛ	t̮	ɪ	k

s	y	m	b	ol
s	ɪ	m	b	l

★**sym·bol** /'sɪmbl/ *noun* [C] **1 a symbol (of sth)** a sign, object, etc. which represents an idea or an aspect of life: *The cross is the symbol of Christianity.* ◇ *Some people think a fast car is a symbol of power and strength.* **2 symbol (for sth)** a letter, number or sign that has a particular meaning: *O is the symbol for oxygen.*

2 a Look at these vowel sounds and practice pronouncing them with the example words on the inside back cover of the **Oxford Dictionary of American English**.

ɪ   aɪ   i   æ   ɛ   u   ʌ   eɪ   ɑ

b Now sort the words below into the table according to their vowel sounds. (Note: not all the blanks will be filled.)

feel	hate	fail	~~sit~~	hat	~~hut~~	fell
dean	dine	sight	~~den~~	height	suit	done
~~file~~	heat	seat	fool	hit	din	sat
hoot	hot	fill	set			

	ɪ	aɪ	i	æ	ɛ	u	ʌ	e	ɑ
st	*sit*								
ht							*hut*		
dn					*den*				
fl		*file*							

c Check your answers in the dictionary.

One of the more difficult aspects of learning to pronounce English words is that words spelled in a similar way can sound different, and words spelled differently can sound similar. The pronunciation guide for each word is particularly useful in these cases.

3 Look up the following pairs of words and read the pronunciation guides to see which pairs of words rhyme (= have the same vowel sound). (Circle) the pairs which rhyme.

a (sum / gum)   **g** fear / near   **m** wood / food
b dumb / hum   **h** bear / dare   **n** wood / hood
c dull / full   **i** their / hare   **o** low / mow
d calm / mom   **j** shall / tall   **p** how / crow
e date / late   **k** wall / ball   **q** dough / cough
f there / here   **l** should / good   **r** rough / tough

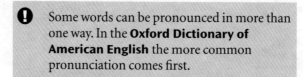

❶   Some words can be pronounced in more than one way. In the **Oxford Dictionary of American English** the more common pronunciation comes first.

4 Look up the following words in the dictionary to find which ones can be pronounced in one way and which in two. Write 1 or 2 next to each word.

a camera _____

b adult _____

c either _____

d imagination _____

e able _____

f aunt _____

g vase _____

h very _____

i route _____

j roof _____

> ❗ Various common words such as *a, an, to,* and *for* have both strong and weak pronunciations. The weak forms are more common (see page 828 of the **Oxford Dictionary of American English** for more information).

5 The words in italics have both strong and weak forms. Read the sentences and decide whether the word should be pronounced in its strong or weak form. Write *S* for *strong* or *W* for *weak*.

a "You dropped *your* ticket." _____ "No, that's *your* ticket, not mine." _____

b "So you were you on your way *to* Biloxi when the car broke down?" _____ "No, we weren't going *to* Biloxi, we were on our way home." _____

c "Is that a letter *from* Beth?" _____ "No it's not *from* her, it's for her." _____

> ❗ Note that most words are pronounced only one way.

6 Match the words on the left with the phonetically spelled words on the right.

left   / læf /

lift   / liv /

leave   / lɛft /

love   / laɪf /

laugh   / lɪft /

loaf   / loʊf /

life   / lʌv /

C Syllables and stress

As mentioned earlier, the pronunciation guide shows how many syllables each word has and which syllables are stressed. The syllables are shown in the headword itself and the stress is shown in the phonetic spelling. Very often students mispronounce words because they stress the wrong syllable.

1 a Read the following words, and draw lines through the word to show the syllables.

▶ example: **in/ter/act**

costume   ornithologist

effective   inconsiderate

heredity

b Look the words up in the dictionary to check your answers.

c Ⓒircle the syllables with primary stress and underline the syllables with secondary stress, where appropriate. example: **in** / ter /Ⓐct

2 Many words have the same form whether they are used as a noun or as a verb. In some cases, however, the nouns are pronounced differently from the verbs. This difference is usually due to the stress being on a different syllable.

Look up the following pairs and:

● put a check (✓) next to the pairs of words which keep the same stress pattern in the noun and the verb form

● underline the stressed syllable in each word of the pairs which change their stress pattern;

The first one has been done for you.

NOUNS	VERBS
produce	produce
✓ review	review
object	object
increase	increase
permit	permit
disguise	disguise
desert	desert
promise	promise
conduct	conduct
cover	cover
conflict	conflict

> ❗ Note that adjectives which are the same form as their verb or noun can also vary in pronunciation, such as the verb/adjective *deliberate* and the noun/adjective *minute.*

D   Spelling

Many students think they can only use a dictionary if they already know how to spell the word they want to look up. However, there are many times when you do not know how to spell the word that you want to look up. This exercise will help you to solve this problem.

Many of the sounds in English can be spelled in different ways. If you cannot find a word because you are not sure how it is spelled, follow these tips:

1   try to spell your word phonetically, using the phonetic symbols on the bottom of the dictionary pages or on the inside back cover of **Oxford Dictionary of American English**

2   check alternate spellings for the phonetic sounds (see examples below)

3   check alternate vowels or vowel combinations

4   check for silent letters such as a final e as in have or b as in *comb*.

Words **beginning** with the following sounds might be spelled with any of the letter combinations shown.

- *c* as in cup = *ch* as in character = *k* as in kind = *qu* as in quiet
- *c* as in circle = *s* as in soda = *ps* as in psychic
- *sh* as in ship = *ch* as in chauvinism
- *sk* as in skate = *sc* as in score = *sch* as in school
- *f* as in forget = *ph* as in phone
- *y* as in you = *u* as in use
- *j* as in judge = *g* as in general
- *n* as in no = *kn* as in knee
- *r* as in red = *wr* as in wrap
- *w* as in west = *wh* as in while
- *wh* as in whole = *h* as in hole

Words **ending** with the following sounds might be spelled with any of the letter combinations shown.

- *-f* as in safe = *-gh* as in laugh
- *z* as in buzz = *s* as in does
- *-ow* as in mow = *-ough* as in dough = *-oe* as in toe = *-o* as in go
- *-y* as in by = *-ie* as in lie = *-igh* as in sigh
- *-ite* as in bite = *-ight* as in fight
- *able* as in manageable = *-ible* as in possible
- *-ate* as in climate = *-it* as in rabbit

---

1   There are lots of ways of pronouncing the letters "-ough".

Look at the words in the circles and check the dictionary to make sure you know how to pronounce them.

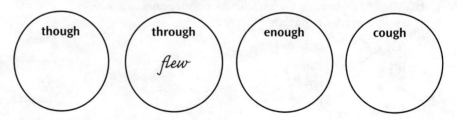

though   through   enough   cough

flew

Now put these words in the circle with the word that they rhyme with (= sound like). The first one has been done for you.

flew   ago   gruff   tattoo   glue   toe   off   tow   cuff

2 Read the following lists of words aloud. In each list, all the words except for one have the same sound at the beginning or end (in *italics*). (Circle) the one word in each list whose *italicized* beginning or ending does not have the same sound as all the other words. The first one has been done for you.

a	defens*ible*	soci*able*	debat*able*	(un*able*)	ed*ible*	negoti*able*	feas*ible*
b	*ch*aos	*k*ind	*q*uick	*k*eep	*c*andy	*ch*orus	*kn*ock
c	*sh*ame	*ch*alet	*ch*eese	*sh*ore	*ch*ampagne	*ch*andelier	*sh*in
d	*y*outh	*u*pset	*y*our	*u*tility	*u*sual	*u*niform	*y*uppie
e	*g*erm	*j*am	*g*eometry	*j*et	*g*ear	*g*entle	*j*ump
f	h*oe*	sh*oe*	st*ow*	th*ough*	f*oe*	cr*ow*	sh*ow*
g	*wh*o	*wh*ite	*w*in	*w*alk	*wh*irl	*wh*isk	*w*ide

3 a Use the guide in the inside back cover of **Oxford Dictionary of American English** to help you pronounce the following words and spell them.

/rʌf/   ————

/ˈdʒɪŋgl/   ————

/ˈklaɪmət/   ————

/eɪk/   ————

/ˈkʌstəm/   ————

/ˈremboʊ/   ————

/zu/   *zoo*

/ˈfɑrməsɪst/   ————

/brɑnz/   ————

/loʊ/   ————

/ˈhæbət/   ————

/ˈskɔrbɔrd/   ————

/tʃeɪs/   ————

/saɪz/   ————

/krʌntʃ/   ————

/dun/   ————

b Check your spellings in the dictionary. Using the spelling tips above to try alternatives if necessary. Put the words into groups according to the number of letters they contain. One of the words has been done for you. Then use these words to fill in the blanks in the puzzle below. Use each word only once.

3 letters: _ _ _ , _ _ _

4 letters: *z o o* _ , _ _ _ _ , _ _ _ _

5 letters: _ _ _ _ _ , _ _ _ _ _ _ , _ _ _ _ _

6 letters: _ _ _ _ _ _ , _ _ _ _ _ _ , _ _ _ _ _ _ _ ,

    _ _ _ _ _ _ ,

7 letters: _ _ _ _ _ _ _ , _ _ _ _ _ _ _ ,

10 letters: _ _ _ _ _ _ _ _ _ _ , _ _ _ _ _ _ _ _ _ _

PART TWO
Topic work

TOPIC 1 Television

1 What's on TV tonight?

Use your dictionary to help you match the following definitions with the kinds of shows on the TV screen

a a program on which people talk about their lives and answer questions, often from the audience

b a story about the lives and problems of a group of people which continues every day or several times a week

c a funny program which shows the same characters in a different situation each week

d a program that gives facts or information about a particular subject

e an advertisement that is as long as a regular program

f a program on which people play games or answer questions in order to win prizes

g a program that tells a story by using moving drawings instead of real people and places

cartoon
documentary
game show
infomercial
sitcom
soap opera
talk show

2 Here are tonight's TV listings.
Which shows are these people most likely to watch?

MARIA, teenager _____

RALPH, police officer _____

FRANCES, senior citizen _____

Channel 4	Channel 5	Channel 9
8:00 Top 10 Hits (music videos)	**8:00** Firearms in our Schools (current affairs)	**8:00** Antique Collecting
8:30 Law Enforcement Update	**8:30** High School, USA (comedy)	
9:00 Cops on the Beat (drama)	**9:00** Cooking in Grandma's Kitchen	**9:00** MOVIE: Prom Night Dreams
10:00 Social Security and Medicare: Your Rights (documentary)	**10:00** Prison Guard (drama)	

3 Here are some useful words and expressions connected with television.
Use them to fill in the blanks in the sentences below.
Use your **Oxford Dictionary of American English** to help you.

broadcast	cable TV	channel	couch potato
satellite	turn off	commercial	remote control
turn up	what's on		

a The Olympics are _____ live by _____ .

b You can _____ the TV. I don't want to watch anything.

c You watch too much TV. I think you're becoming a real _____ .

d I'll _____ the TV if you can't hear it. Where's the _____?

e I think I'll stay home tonight. Do you know _____ TV?

f Which _____ is that movie on?

g We have a bigger choice of shows to watch now that we have _____ .

h I saw a _____ for a new brand of bubble gum today.

TOPIC 2 Sports

1 Can you group these sports into the categories below? Some of them will fit into more than one category.

aerobics	ice skating	swimming
baseball	jogging	table tennis
basketball	skateboarding	tennis
football	skiing	volleyball
golf	snowboarding	weightlifting
gymnastics	soccer	windsurfing
hockey	softball	

sports played outdoors

sports played with a ball

sports played with a racket, paddle, or bat

sports played indoors

sports played on a team

sports played with a net

sports played in cold weather

sports played in water

2 Here are some other useful words connected with sports. Can you match the words with their definitions?

coach	referee	stadium
court	ice rink	tournament
field	spectators	umpire
match		

a a person who watches a game such as baseball or tennis to make sure that the players obey the rules

_____

b an area where certain ball games are played, such as basketball or tennis

_____

c a large sports ground with rows of seats around it

_____

d a person who controls a football or soccer game and prevents the rules from being broken

_____

e the people who watch a sports game, a show, etc.

_____

f an organized game of tennis

_____

g a person who trains people to compete in sports

_____

h an area of land where you can play sports, such as football or baseball

_____

i a large area of ice that people can skate or play hockey on

_____

j a competition in which many players or teams play against each other

_____

Check your answers in your dictionary.

3 Club, racket, stick or bat?

Fill in the blanks with the correct words. Check your answers by looking up the words in **dark type**.

a You play **golf** with a _____ .

b You play **hockey** with a _____ .

c You play **baseball** with a _____ .

d You play **tennis** with a _____ .

TOPIC 3 Shapes

1 Can you label these shapes?
Use the words from the box.

circle	triangle
square	oval
crescent	diamond
rectangle	star

_____   _____   _____   _____

Check your answers in your
dictionary.

_____   _____   _____   _____

2 Fill in the adjectives in
the table below.

noun	adjective
circle	*round or*
triangle	
rectangle	
square	
oval	

3 What shapes are these objects?
Use adjectives to describe them.

a postcard _____

an egg _____

your dictionary _____

dice _____

a dinner plate _____

your eyes _____

a floppy disk _____

4 Dimensions

a Using your dictionary, fill in the table below.

noun	adjectives	
		opposite
length		
	broad	
		shallow
	/high	

b **Tall** and **high** are not used in exactly the same
way. Which would you use with the words below?
Check your answers in your dictionary.

a _____ woman

a _____ brick wall

a _____ mountain

a _____ pine tree

5 Put the correct adjective in these questions.

a "How _____ are you?"

"Five foot seven."

b "How _____ is this swimming pool?"

"Only four feet. You can't dive into it."

c How _____ is the fence?

Could someone climb over it?

d How _____ is the creek?

Can we jump across?

TOPIC 4 Cooking

1 What's cooking?

A Here are some useful words connected with cooking. Can you match the words with their definitions?

boil	broil	chop	roast	defrost
fry	peel	slice	blend	

a to cook something under a heat source in an oven, or on a frame of metal bars over flames _____

b to cut something into small pieces _____

c to mix together _____

d to cut something into flat pieces _____

e to take the skin off a fruit or vegetable _____

f to heat a liquid to a high temperature where bubbles rise to the surface and the liquid changes to a gas _____

g to cook something in an oven or over a fire

_____

h to cook something in hot fat or oil _____

i to bring something to a normal temperature again after freezing _____

B Look up the words in the box above in your dictionary to check your answers. How many of the words can also be used as nouns? Write them in the space below.

_____

C Now fill in the blanks with the nouns from your list.

a Careful don't step on that banana _____ !

b She put some butter on a _____ of bread.

c Dad bought a big beef _____ for the whole family's dinner.

d Bring the water to a _____ before you put the spaghetti in.

e This tea is a _____ of several types of leaves.

f Are you hungry enough to eat two pork _____ s for supper?

2 Making chocolate chip cookies

Chocolate chip cookies are a favorite treat. These are the ingredients that go into the cookies:

> 1 c. margarine or butter
> ¾ c. sugar
> ¾ c. packed brown sugar
> 1 egg
> 2¼ c. all-purpose flour
> 1 tsp. baking soda
> ½ tsp. salt
> 1 c. chopped nuts (optional)
> 1 bag (12 oz.) chocolate chips

Make sure you know what the measurements are by checking the abbreviations in your **Oxford Dictionary of American English**. (Remember: they are in alphabetical order like other words.) Then look at the recipe below. You will find that some of the verbs are missing – they are in the box. Look up their meanings in your dictionary and decide where to put them into the recipe to fill in the blanks.

bake	cool	drop	preheat	mix
remove	soften	stir	store	

(**a**) _____ the oven to 375° F.

Leave the margarine or butter at room temperature for a while to (**b**) _____ . In a large bowl,

(**c**) _____ the margarine or butter, sugar, brown sugar, and egg. Use a large wooden spoon to

(**d**) _____ in the flour, baking soda, and salt.

Add the nuts and chocolate chips. (**e**) _____ the dough in large teaspoonfuls about 2 inches apart onto an ungreased cookie sheet. (**f**) _____ until light brown, about 8 to 10 minutes.

Take the cookies from the oven and let them

(**g**) _____ slightly. (**h**) _____ the cookies from the cookie sheet. (**i**) _____ the cookies in an airtight container.

TOPIC 5 Food and shopping

1 Groceries

Look at the picture at **container** in your **Oxford Dictionary of American English** and make sure that you know all the words there. Then close your dictionary and fill in the blanks on the shopping list with the correct items from the list below.

chocolates	cola
jam	milk
potato chips	toothpaste
water	

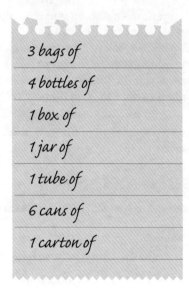

3 bags of

4 bottles of

1 box of

1 jar of

1 tube of

6 cans of

1 carton of

2 On a diet

Each of these people is on a different type of diet.
Write the foods from the list that each person should avoid.
Look up the words in **dark type** to help you.

bacon	low-fat yogurt	home fries	fish
potato chips	caffè latte	fried chicken	skim milk
chef's salad	ice cream		

Fred is on a **diet**.	Amy is **allergic** to **dairy** products.	Sam is a **vegetarian**.

3 Ethnic food

A lot of the food people enjoy eating in North America originally comes from other countries. Match the following kinds of food and drink with the place they come from, using the definitions in your dictionary to help you.

curry	Mexico
lasagna	Africa
tortilla	China
sushi	Italy
pumpernickel	India
dim sum	Spain
egg roll	Germany
couscous	Mexico
sangria	China
ciabatta	Japan
quesadilla	Italy

4 Talking shop

Read the definitions below and fill in the blanks with **store** or **shop**.

a a place that sells food, magazines and other small items, and stays open until late at night

a convenience _____

b a place that sells medicine, soap, shampoo, film, etc.

a drug _____

c to steal something from a store while pretending to be a customer

to _____ **lift**

d a place where things are made or repaired

a work _____

e a room where things are kept until they are needed

a _____ **room**

f a factory where people are forced to work very hard in poor conditions for very little money, often illegally

a sweat _____

g a large basket on wheels that you push around in a store and put things into

a _____ **ping cart**

Check your answers in your **Oxford Dictionary of American English**.

TOPIC 6 Clothes

1 These people like to wear a lot of patterns at the same time. Look at the illustration on page A30 of your **Oxford Dictionary of American English** and fill in the blanks to describe the patterns they are wearing.

▶ *Jill is wearing a _____ blouse and a _____ skirt.*

▶ *Liz is wearing a _____ sweater and _____ pants.*

▶ *Marvin is wearing a _____ shirt and a _____ tie.*

2 Look at the pictures below and choose the right answers.

▶ *Tom's sweater is too big/not big enough.*

▶ *Kevin's sweater is too big/not big enough.*

Check your answers by looking at the picture at the entry for **too** on page 732 of your dictionary.

3 Look at the pictures and fill in the name of each item in the puzzle to reveal the name of a piece of clothing.

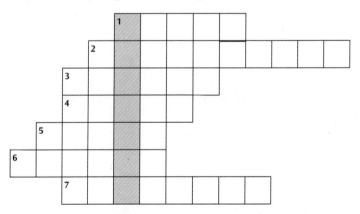

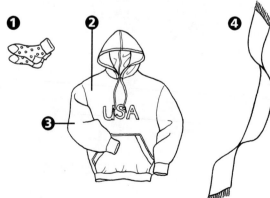 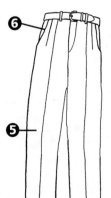

TOPIC 7 Apartment hunting

1 Look at the note at the entry for **apartment** in your dictionary. It contains some useful words connected with apartments. Close your dictionary. Can you match the words with their definitions?

deposit	landlord	rent
roommate	superintendent	tenant

a a person or company that rents a house or an apartment to people for money

_____

b a person who pays rent to the owner of an apartment, so that he/she can live in it

_____

c money that you pay regularly for the use of a house or an apartment

_____

d a person who is in charge of a building and makes small repairs, etc. to it

_____

e a sum of money that you pay when you rent something and that you get back when you return it or finish using it without damage

_____

f a person you share a room or an apartment with

_____

2 Moving in

Look at page **A31** in the study pages and make sure you know all the words for the rooms in a house. Then list these pieces of furniture and other items under the name of the room where you would probably find them in a house or an apartment. Some of the items may be used in more than one room. Check any unknown words in the main part of the dictionary.

armchair	bathtub	bed	bookcase
coffee table	couch	dresser	dishwasher
mattress	shower	sink	refrigerator
stove	toilet		

LIVING ROOM

_____

_____

_____

_____

KITCHEN

_____

_____

_____

_____

BEDROOM

_____

_____

_____

_____

BATHROOM

_____

_____

_____

_____

TOPIC 8 Health and fitness

1 Without looking at a dictionary, label the following parts of the body.

shin	ankle
shoulder	calf
stomach	elbow
thigh	heel
sole	hip
toes	waist
wrist	thumb

Now look at the picture on page **A32** of your dictionary to check if you were right.

2 Here are some useful words connected with health and medical care. Use them to fill in the blanks in the sentences below. Use your dictionary to help you.

clinic	HMO	nurse	emergency room
orthodontist	patient	surgery	health insurance

a When I start my new job, I can apply to become

a member of an _____

b "Did you have to pay for the treatment yourself?"

"No, I have_____."

c That looks like a serious injury. We'd better take him to the

_____ .

d The _____ came into the room and took my

temperature.

e My doctor says I might need _____ on my knee.

f I have an appointment to see a doctor at our neighborhood

_____ .

g Grandma is recovering from a serious illness. She's a

_____ at the Brown County Hospital.

h My son has to go to the _____ to have his teeth

straightened.

3 Look up the names of these illnesses in your dictionary and make sure you know how to say them. Underline the part of each word that has the main stress. Then close your book and with a partner practice spelling the words.

▶ *Example:* Student A "How do you spell laryngitis?"
Student B "L-A-R-Y-N-G-I-T-I-S"

arthritis	cholera	leukemia	tonsillitis
bronchitis	diarrhea	measles	whooping cough
chicken pox	laryngitis	schizophrenia	

4 Label the illustration using the words in the box.

sling
Band-Aid™
IV
dressing
plaster cast
bandage

5 What is it, doctor?

Dr. Dither doesn't like to make a diagnosis in a hurry. He likes to consider the possibilities when patients describe their symptoms. Look again at the list of illnesses in the box and use some of them to fill in the blanks in what the doctor says. If you have forgotten what they mean, check again in your dictionary.

a Tom has red spots all over his skin, and he has a fever.
DR. DITHER:
"Well, it could be _____, or it could be _____."

b Alison has a sore throat and can hardly talk.
DR. DITHER:
"It could be _____, or possibly _____."

c Brian has a bad cough.
DR. DITHER:
"You may have _____, or it could be _____."

d Mrs. Wilson has a bad stomachache and has to go to the bathroom a lot.
DR. DITHER:
"It could be _____, or maybe_____ ."

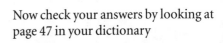

Now check your answers by looking at page 47 in your dictionary

TOPIC 9 Business

1 Match each job on the left with a job activity on the right.
If you are not sure, check the definition in your dictionary.
The first one has been done for you.

a accountant   1 buys and sells things

b tycoon   2 keeps the accounts of the money that a company, etc. spends or receives

c contractor

d bookkeeper   3 is very successful in business and is rich and powerful

e consultant   4 gives advice to people on business, law, etc.

f agent   5 keeps or examines the financial records of a business

g administrator 6 arranges the buying and selling of things such as property, insurance, etc. for other people

h dealer

i proprietor   7 owns a business

j broker   8 organizes or manages a system, a business, etc.

                 9 does business for a company or for another person

                 10 does work, especially building work, by contract

2 Below are some business activities. In pairs decide which ones are involved in each job from **exercise 1**.

- **negotiating contracts**
- **buying shares**
- **marketing goods or services**
- **writing minutes**
- **selling services**
- **preparing invoices for customers selling goods**
- **offering advice**
- **chairing meetings**

TOPIC 10 Your personality

Personality Quiz

What kind of student are you? Answer these quiz questions to find out!
For each question, choose the option which you think best describes you.
When you are finished, use the key to find out your score, and then read
on to find out what kind of student you really are!

❗ Most of the **a**, **b**, and **c** choices contain phrasal verbs which you will need to understand in order to make your choice. Look up any phrasal verbs you don't know in your **Oxford Dictionary of American English**.

1 **You have a long homework assignment which is due next week. Do you:**

a **get down to** it right away?
b **put** it **off** for a couple of days so you have a chance to **think** it **over**?
c check your calendar, because you can't always **fit** homework **into** your busy social life?

2 **You think one of your classmates is cheating on a test. Do you:**

a **tell on** him or her? It's not fair – you had to work hard.
b **get on with** your own test? You need to concentrate.
c **get back to** doodling on your test paper, because you don't care?

3 You have missed several English classes because you were sick. Do you:

a ask another student or your teacher to sit down with you and **go over** the important things you missed?

b worry about it so much that you **come down with** another illness?

c figure that you'll just **pick up** anything important as you **go along**?

4 You have been invited to spend a week with a friend in another city. It will mean missing several of your English classes. Do you:

a **turn down** the invitation right away, because you don't want to **get behind**?

b **jump at** the chance, because you can always **make up for** it later?

c **work out** the pros and cons before making your decision?

5 You have a hard time learning new vocabulary. Do you...

a **give up** and decide to learn an easier language?

b **put together** a vocabulary notebook in which you can **jot down** meanings, example sentences, and other useful information?

c spend hours **drawing up** lists of all the new words with translations of every one in your own language?

6 You come across a new word in an article you are reading. Do you...

a try to **figure out** the meaning from the context and then check in the dictionary if necessary?

b **keep on** reading – you're not **taking** much **in** anyway?

c **look** it **up** right away?

7 You're thinking of buying a new English dictionary. Do you:

a **check out** the features of a few different dictionaries in the bookstore?

b **talk** it **over** with your teacher and see what he or she recommends?

c go and **pick up** the first one you see, because they're probably all the same?

8 You're thinking about taking another English course. How do you find the best one for you? Do you:

a **sign up for** the same one your friend did?

b **call up** several schools and colleges and **pore over** all the various options?

c **write down** exactly what you want and can afford, and then ask your teacher, family, or friends for advice?

Key

1	a 3	b 2	c 1
2	a 3	b 2	c 1
3	a 2	b 3	c 1
4	a 3	b 1	c 2
5	a 1	b 2	c 3
6	a 2	b 1	c 3
7	a 2	b 3	c 1
8	a 1	b 3	c 2

Score

20–24

Be careful – all work and no play isn't good for you! You need to relax a little more, go for a walk, call a friend, or take an evening off. Studying when you're tired or stressed can be unproductive in the long run.

14–20

You seem to have a well-balanced approach to your studies. You work hard without letting your studies take over your life. Keep up the good work!

Under 14

Studying seems to come pretty low on your list of priorities! Try setting aside some regular time for work – you might even enjoy it!

TOPIC 11 The family tree

1 Family tree

Read the statements below about Kristin and her family. Then draw a picture of Kristin's family tree. Check any words you do not know in your **Oxford Dictionary of American English**.

- Kristin has one brother, whose name is Tom.
- Tom's parents are John and Sarah.
- Sarah has a brother and a sister.
- John doesn't have any brothers or sisters.
- John's brother-in-law is named David.
- Nancy, who doesn't have any children, is Kristin's aunt.
- Nancy's father's name is Edward.
- Edward has five grandchildren.
- Tom and Jack are Nancy's nephews.
- Barbara is Edward's wife.
- Ashley and Kendra are Barbara's granddaughters.

Now answer these questions based on Kristin's family tree:

a What relation is Ashley to Kristin?

b What is the relationship between John and Barbara?

c What is the relationship between Sarah and Kendra?

2

Here are some useful words connected with families and relations. Use them to fill in the blanks in the sentences below. Use your dictionary to help you.

ancestor	descendant	generation
next of kin	only child	single parent

a Nicole says she's a _____ of one of the original settlers in this area.

b Mom says that people in her _____ didn't have to worry about things when they were kids.

c The man in that old picture is an _____ of mine – I think he was my great-grandfather.

d We cannot tell reporters the murder victim's name until we have notified his _____.

e Kelly is raising her three kids all by herself – she says it's tough being a _____ .

f "Do you have any brothers or sisters?" "No, I'm an _____ ."

TOPIC 12 Driving and vehicles

1 On the road

What do these road signs mean? Circle the right answer for each one. Use your dictionary to help you understand the words on the signs.

1 a Follow this sign because the road ahead is closed.
b Follow this sign for a scenic tour of the local area.

2 a You must not drive past this sign.
b You must not pass another car that is going in the same direction.

3 a A train track crosses the surface of the road here.
b You can get on a train at a train station here.

4 a You must let cars on the other road go first.
b You have the right to go in front of cars on the other road.

5 a You must drive at least 50 miles per hour.
b You must not drive more than 50 miles per hour.

6 a It is never OK to park here.
b You can park here whenever you want.

2 Here are some useful words connected with driving. Use them to fill in the blanks in the sentences on the right. Use your dictionary to help you.

gas station	headlights
honk	roadkill
seat belt	speeding
steer	trunk
turn signal	driver's license

a "Yuck! What's that smell?" "There's some _____ on the highway – it looks like a dead skunk."

b You might have to show your _____ as identification.

c We're running low on fuel. I hope there's a _____ nearby.

d It's getting dark. You'd better turn on your _____ .

e I thought that guy was going to go straight ahead – he didn't have his _____ on.

f Will all of these suitcases fit into the _____ ?

g You need to fasten your _____ – it's the law.

h That car is blocking our way – _____ your horn at him.

i Don't put your arm out the window. You should use both hands to _____ .

j Brenda got a ticket for _____ yesterday – she was going 75 miles an hour.

3 Look at the pictures at **car** and **truck** in your **Oxford Dictionary of American English** and make sure that you know all the words there. Then close your dictionary and fill in the names of these types of vehicles.

TOPIC 13 Tools

1 Match the names of the tools listed on the left with the pictures below.

drill
hammer
pliers
saw
chisel
screwdriver
wrench

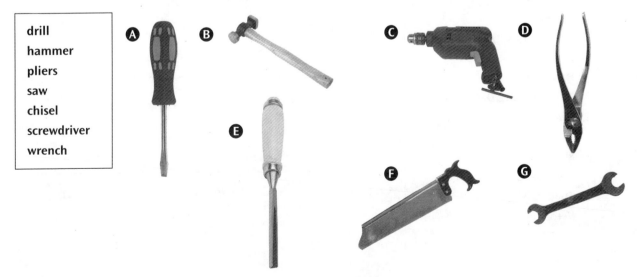

2 Now match the names of the tools with the definitions below.

a _____ a metal tool with an end shaped so that it can be used for turning nuts

b _____ a tool that is used for cutting wood

c _____ a tool with a sharp end that is used for cutting or shaping wood, stone, etc.

d _____ a tool with a heavy metal head that is used for hitting nails

e _____ a tool that is used for holding things tightly, bending things, etc.

f _____ a tool that is used for turning screws

g _____ a tool that is used for making holes in things

Check your answers in your dictionary.

3 Cutting and fastening

Look at the verbs in the box. Are they used for 'cutting' or 'fastening'? Put them into the correct columns.

attach	chop	glue	rip
slice	staple	stick	tear

CUTTING   FASTENING

_____   _____

_____   _____

_____   _____

_____   _____

_____   _____

TOPIC 14   Holidays and celebrations

1 Write these holidays and other special days in the correct months on the calendar. The entries in your **Oxford Dictionary of American English** will help you check when they occur.

April Fool's Day
Christmas
Father's Day
Groundhog Day
Halloween
Hanukkah
Independence Day
Kwanzaa
Labor Day
St. Patrick's Day
New Year's Day
Thanksgiving
Veterans Day

January	February	March
April *April Fool's day*	May	June
July	August	September
October	November	December

2 Here are some things that are connected with certain holidays and other special days. Can you match the words with the names of the days?

eggs	hearts	jack-o'-lanterns
practical jokes		pumpkin pie

a Easter _____

b April Fool's Day _____

c Valentine's Day _____

d Thanksgiving _____

e Halloween _____

3 You can buy many different types of greeting cards for different occasions. Can you match these greeting cards with the most suitable occasion for sending each one?

Christmas _____

a friend's graduation from college _____

a friend's birthday _____

the death of a friend's parent _____

Valentine's Day _____

a baby shower _____

your parents' anniversary _____

a friend is in the hospital _____

TOPIC 15 The weather

1 What's the weather like?

Use your dictionary to look up these words that refer to the weather and decide where to put them on the diagram.

blizzard	breeze	chilly	drizzle
frost	gale	hail	hurricane
monsoon	muggy	sleet	snow
tornado	typhoon		

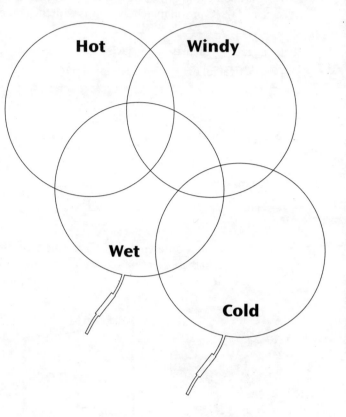

Hot Windy Wet Cold

2 Which words go together? Use your dictionary to help you choose the right words to fill in the blanks.

a a _____ frost (hard/strong)

b _____ fog (deep/dense)

c _____ hot (boiling/cooking)

d It's raining _____ (hard/thickly)

e a _____ wind (strong/tough)

TOPIC 16 Animals

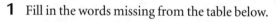

1 Fill in the words missing from the table below.

general name	female	male	young
			puppy
		tomcat	
horse			
		buck	
duck			
			lamb
	hen		

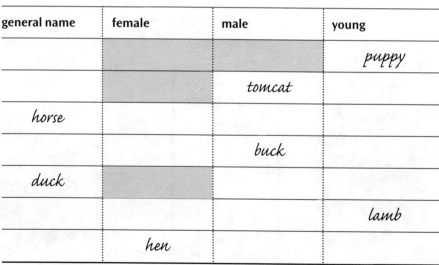

2 List the names of these animals under the categories which describe them. Some of the animals may be used in more than one column.

alligator	flamingo	squirrel
beaver	octopus	worm
mouse	shark	

has a long tail	has fur	has sharp teeth	doesn't have any legs	lives in or near water

Check your answers in your dictionary.

3 Match these animals with the sounds that they make.

sheep	buzz
bee	roar
bird	chirp
cat	baa
cow	quack
horse	meow
duck	neigh
lion	moo

4 Use the pictures in the A-Z section of the **Oxford Dictionary of American English** to name these animals. The first letter has been given to help you.

d	a	t	l

d	s	k

TOPIC 17 Work

1 In pairs, look at the list of jobs below. Practice saying the words aloud and then underline the stressed syllable in each of them like this: <u>ac</u>tor. Use your dictionary to check your answers.

<u>ac</u>tor	electrician	engineer	farmer
firefighter	garbage man	journalist	librarian
nanny	midwife	miner	politician
podiatrist	programmer	psychiatrist	surgeon
teacher	waiter		

Now choose eight jobs from the list which you believe should be the best paid. Then compare lists with your partner. How much do you both agree? Explain the reasons for your choices.

2 In the column on the left is a list of tools (1–8) used in the jobs listed on the right (a–h). Using your dictionary to help you, see how quickly you can match them.

1 a hoe and a rake   a a nurse
2 a mop, a bucket and a sponge   b a carpenter
3 a spatula, a spoon and a whisk   c a photographer
4 scissors and a hair dryer   d a hairdresser
5 a scalpel and a pair of forceps   e a surgeon
6 a syringe and a thermometer   f a chef
7 a chisel, a hammer and a saw   g a gardener
8 a tripod and a zoom lens   h a cleaner

3 Look at the adjectives below and use your dictionary to check the meaning of any that you do not know. Then, with your partner, decide which adjective(s) could describe either the job, or the person doing the job, in the list that follows. Give reasons for your choice of adjective(s). Your opinions may vary.

worthwhile	challenging	high-powered	blue-collar
skilled	demanding	mundane	white-collar
manual	stressful	menial	underpaid
sedentary			

an astronaut	a secretary	an air traffic controller
a factory worker	a cleaner	a hairdresser
a letter carrier	a builder	a nurse
a lawyer	a charity worker	a teacher
a pediatrician	a company president	

4 Take turns with your partner to choose one of the jobs mentioned in the exercises in this section. Keep your choice a secret. Your partner now has ten questions to find out what the job is. You may only answer yes or no.

Example (a doctor)

STUDENT A: Do you earn a lot of money?
STUDENT B: Yes.
STUDENT A: Is your job challenging?
STUDENT B: Yes.
STUDENT A: Do you use a camera and tripod?
STUDENT B: No.

TOPIC 18 Crime and the law

1 In pairs or groups discuss who the following people are and what they do in a court of law:

> the judge   the defendant
>
> the jury   witnesses

2 Match the verbs on the left below with the words on the right and then decide which of the people in exercise 1 does each of these things in court. You may only use each word or phrase once. The first one has been done for you.

plead	verdict
cross-examine	sentence
return	guilty or not guilty
pass	defendant
acquit or convict	witnesses

3 Now using your answers from exercises **1** and **2** decide on the order in which each of these things might happen during a trial. You will need to change the form of the verbs to make full sentences. The first one has been done for you.

1 *The defendant pleads guilty or not guilty.* _____
2 _____
3 _____
4 _____
5 _____

4 Silence in court!

Legal language is not only difficult to understand – it is often difficult to pronounce, too. In each of the words below, there is a letter which is not spoken. Look up the pronunciation of these words in your **Oxford Dictionary of American English** and <u>underline</u> the silent letter in each one.

arraign

guilty

indictment

subpoena

writ

TOPIC 19 Computers

1 Parts of the computer

Read through study page **A27** in your **Oxford Dictionary of American English** and make sure you know the names of the parts of a computer shown on the illustration there. Then close your dictionary and fill in the missing letters in these words:

s ___ r ___ e ___

m ___ ___ s ___

m ___ n ___ ___ ___ ___

p ___ ___ ___ t e ___

k ___ ___ b ___ ___ r ___

D ___ ___ - ___ ___ ___ d ___ ___ ___ ___

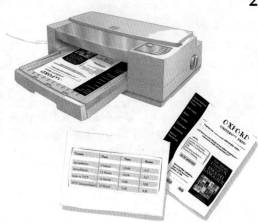

2 Match the following words with their definitions:

1 **attachment**

2 **dialog box**

3 **double-click**

4 **IMHO**

5 **Webcam™**

a a box that appears on a computer screen asking the user to choose what he/she wants to do next

b the abbreviation for "in my humble opinion", used especially in Internet chat rooms

c a video camera connected to a computer so that what it records can be seen on a website as it happens

d to choose a particular function or item on a computer screen by pressing one of the mouse buttons twice quickly

e a document that you send to somebody with an e-mail message

3 Look at the words in the box and make sure you know what they mean. Use your dictionary if there are any you are not sure about. Then use words from the box to fill the blanks in the text.

e-zine

computer-literate

Internet café

DVD   surfing

downloaded   hyperlink

dotcom   URLs

ISP

e-businesses

bookmarking

sites

favorites   e-mail

information superhighway

bounce

Web

emoticon

My grandmother called me last week. She said that although she had never used a computer, she wanted to get onto the **(1)** _____, so she was going to go to an **(2)** _____ with a **(3)** _____ friend. It turned out to be a lot easier than Grandma had expected. First she found an **(4)** _____ for senior citizens and **(5)** _____ a couple of interesting articles. From that page she followed a **(6)** _____ and found an exercise class for older people in her town. Then she ordered a birthday present for a friend from a **(7)** _____ . Grandma says that **(8)** _____ can be a big help for older people who can't always get out of the house. In fact, she liked it so much that she went out and bought a new computer (with a **(9)** _____ player!) and signed up with an **(10)** _____ . For the past week she's started each day with a cup of coffee at the computer, **(11)** _____ the **(12)** _____ and **(13)** _____ the **(14)** _____ of the **(15)** _____ she likes best to her **(16)** _____ folder. How do I know all this? I just got an **(17)** _____ from Grandma. She wrote "I hope I have your address right and this message doesn't **(18)** _____ ." And then she had put in an **(19)** _____ :-) !

Answer Key

1 Introducing the Oxford Dictionary of American English

A Answers will vary.

B 1a 1 (circled headwords) dire, direct
   2 1
   3 because there is another entry for "direct" – a verb
   4 (underlined words)
   5 (boxed words)
   6 diplomatically
   7 2
   8 2

   1b 1 verb
   2 pump iron
   3 up
   4 bicycle; shoe
   5 note

dip·lo·mat·ic /ˌdɪpləˈmætɪk/ *adj.* **1** connected with DIPLOMACY (1): *Diplomatic relations between the two countries have been restored.* **2** clever at dealing with people: *He searched for a diplomatic reply so as not to offend her.* ▶ **dip·lo·mat·i·cal·ly** /-kli/ *adv.*

dire /ˈdaɪər/ *adj.* (*formal*) very bad or serious; terrible: *dire consequences* ◇ *dire poverty*

di·rect /dəˈrɛkt; daɪ-/ *adj.* **1** going from one place to another without turning or stopping; straight: *The most direct route is through the center of town.* ◇ *a direct flight to Hong Kong* **2** with nobody/nothing in between; not involving anybody/anything else: *The President is in direct contact with his Cabinet.* ◇ *Keep the plant away from direct sunlight.* **3** saying what you mean; clear: *Politicians never give a direct answer to a direct question.* [OPP] The opposite for senses **1**, **2** and **3** is **indirect 4** (only *before* a noun) complete; exact: *What she did was in direct opposition to my orders.*

C To find the correct spelling of a word – headwords

To find the meaning of a word – meanings; explanations; illustrations; shortcuts

To find the pronunciation of a word – pronunciation guides

To find the appropriate use of a word – notes; examples; grammar information; guides to formality

D

Crossword:
1 PAST
7 TRANSITIVE
10 OPPOSITE
12 UNCOUNTABLE
13 ADVERB
15 PRESENT
17 SINGULAR

2 Finding words quickly

A 1a beech, cedar, fir, hickory, magnolia, yew
   blog, freeware, palmtop, spellchecker, Webmaster

   b Group 1: kinds of tree.
   Group 2: words connected with I.T. or computers.

   3 Alex couldn't sleep very well. Betsy hadn't returned yet. Candles flickered in the wind. Darkness enveloped his room. He hoped she'd show up.

B line 1   lip 6   list 9   liqueur 7
   link 4   literature 12   literate 11   lion 5
   listen 10   liquid 8   lining 3   liner 2

C 1a find → finish; freshen → frisk; front → fuel; function → furnished; getaway → girlfriend; godfather → good.

   1b, and 2a

   1 find → finish:
   finding
   fine
   finely
   fingertip

   2 freshen → frisk:
   friction
   friendly
   frighten
   frilly

   3 front → fuel:
   fruitful
   frustration
   fry
   fudge

   4 function → furnished:
   fungus
   funky
   funny
   furious

   5 getaway → girlfriend:
   ghost
   gingerbread
   gingham
   giraffe

   6 godfather → good:
   gofer
   goggles
   gold
   gone

D fire engine 6   firefighter 8
   fire 1   fire department 5
   firearm 3   fire extinguisher 7
   fire alarm 2   fire cracker 4

E duty-free 2   IPA – language learning
   dwarf 4   IA – science
   duty 1   VP – politics
   DVD 3   ISP – computers
             UPC – shopping
             RX – health

F 1 presidential: president
   prettily: pretty
   protester: protest
   rapidity: rapid
   realization: realize
   substitution: substitute
   half-heartedly: half-hearted
   doubtfully: doubtful
   confiscation: confiscate
   anorexic: anorexia

   2 traveled: travel
   asking: ask
   waits: wait
   looking: look
   hated: hate
   stones: stone
   weighing: weigh
   disks: disk
   friskier: frisky
   handymen: handyman
   slipping: slip

3 Idioms and Phrasal Verbs

A a 2 – chest   d 1 – ears   g 10 – eye   j 5 – back
   b 6 – head   e 11 – feet   h 4 – arm   k 8 – mind
   c 3 – nose   f 7 – heart   i 9 – head… heels

B 1 Could you **keep an eye on** my bags for me while I go into the store, please?
   2 …I don't want your mother **sticking her nose in**!
   3 Mark and Emma are both still **head over heels in love** even after five years.
   4 …at the last minute he **got cold feet** and decided to keep quiet.
   5 …It might do you good to **get it off your chest**.
   6 …See if you can **twist her arm**.
   7 You'll just have to **make up your mind** which one you want.
   8 When I asked him what he wanted to eat, he just **bit my head off**.
   9 It's not fair of us to discuss Jo's work **behind her back**.
   10 We're too busy because we just moved house and we**'re up to our ears in** boxes that need unpacking.

C a be an old hand (at sth)
b change hands
c out of hand
d on hand
e get the upper hand

D **back** – in return
on – continuing
off – separate, no longer attached

E 1 back 2 off 3 on 4 back 5 on 6 off

F turn sth on – turn sth off   pick sth up – put sth down
put sth on – take sth off   cheer sb up – get sb down
check in – check out   pull over – pull out
give up – take up   pick sb up – drop sb off

G add – up   a perked up
plug – in   b added up
weigh – down   c weighed down
perk – up   d plug in

4 Finding the right meaning

A 1 bake sale – event   snowmobile – vehicle
enchilada – dish   cold-calling – practice
snowblower – machine   personal trainer – person
Botox – substance   spandex – material
paragliding – sport

3 a asbestos   d elevator   g camper
b beggar   e tragedy   h satay
c honey   f wrestling   i vivisection

C 1 chest, definition 1   7 arm, entry 2, definition 1
2 head, entry 2, definition 1   8 calf, definition 1
3 mouth, entry 1, definition 2   9 hand, entry 2, definition 1
4 foot, entry 1, definition 6   10 leg, definition 4
5 sole, entry 2, definition 3   11 eye, entry 1, definition 3
6 hip, entry2, definition 1   12 shoulder, entry 2, definition 1

D 1a 2   e the note in parentheses
b adjective and verb   f verb
c adjective   g 3
d 2   h [T]

2a 4 c 1 e 5 g 4 i 1 k 5
b 6 d 7 f 2 h 6 j 2

5 Word families

A 1 **noun**
Definition: a word that is the name of a person, place, thing
or idea.
EXAMPLE: *Those **words** are hard to understand.*

verb
Definition: a word or group of words that is used to indicate an
action or state
EXAMPLE: *We **are** students.*

adjective
Definition: a word used with a noun that tells you more about it.
EXAMPLE: *All the **best** students got above 90% on the test.*

adverb
Definition: a word that adds information to a verb, adjective,
phrase, or adverb.
EXAMPLE: *The cat and dog glared at each other **angrily**.*

	noun	verb	adjective	adverb	similar in meaning	different in meaning
fake	✓	✓	✓		1,2,3	
gaze	✓	✓			1,2	
marvel	✓	✓			1,2	
inside	✓		✓	✓	1,2,3	
express		✓	✓	v	2,3	1
fair	✓		✓	✓	1,2	3
light	✓	✓	✓	✓	1,2	3,4
prompt	✓	✓	✓			1,2,3
chow	✓	✓			1,2	
forward	✓	✓	✓	✓	1,2	3,4

5a boxed: 1,3,9,12,14
circled: 2,5,8,11,13
checked: 4,6,7,10,15

B 2a

im-	impolite	impure	
un-	ungrateful		
ir-	irrational	irresponsible	
in-	insensitive	inadequate	intolerant
il-	illegible	illogical	
dis-	disobedient	dishonest	

c

-er	trainer	employer	teacher
-or	director	actor	creator
-ist	scientist	artist	
-ian	musician	electrician	comedian
-ee	trainee	employee	
-ant	attendant	assistant	accountant

3a

C 1a (underlined words): blizzard, dangerous, alarmed, serious, undeterred, seemingly, terrified, outage, endless, modest

   b **blackout** – outage
    snowstorm – blizzard
    grave – serious
    apparently – seemingly
    undaunted – undeterred
    perilous – dangerous
    petrified – terrified
    interminable – endless
    self-effacing – modest

  2a-b
    opposites:
    success – failure
    accurate – inaccurate
    possible – impossible
    advantage – disadvantage
    increase – reduce
    cheap – expensive
    comfortable – uncomfortable
    convenient – inconvenient
    efficient – inefficient
    suitable – unsuitable
    popular – unpopular
    approve – disapprove
    satisfactory – unsatisfactory

6 Using information about grammar and usage

A 1a 1 **mouse** – [C] (*pl.* mice)
    2 **eyeglasses** – [plural]
    3 **candidacy** – [U]
    4 **the Irish** – [plural]
    5 **knowledge** – [U, sing.]
    6 **the last** – [C] (*pl.* last) **the last (of sb/sth)**
    7 **restriction** – **restriction (on sth)**

   1b 1 ~~mouses~~ mice
    2 ~~eyeglass~~ eyeglasses
    3 ~~candidacies~~ candidacy
    4 ~~Irish~~ Irishman
    5 ~~knowledges~~ knowledge
    6 ~~the lasts~~ the last
    7 ~~a restriction in~~ a restriction on

B 1a 1 disturb [T]
    2 qualify (*pres. part.* **qualifying**; *3rd pers. sing. pres.* **qualifies**; *p.t., p.p.* **qualified**)
    3 ban (**banning; banned**) [T]
    4 subsist [I]
    5 acquaint [T] **acquaint sb/yourself with sth**
    6 undo [T] (*3rd pers sing pres* **undoes**; *pt* **undid**; *pp* **undone**)
    7 look sth up (separable)

   b 1 Oh sorry! I didn't mean to *disturb you.*
    2 She hopes to get a job in computer programming when she *qualifies.*
    3 Both athletes may be *banned* from taking part in the Olympics.
    4 Their families *subsist* on rice and a few vegetables.
    5 She wanted to *acquaint* herself with the area.
    6 Sam's mistake *undid* all his previous efforts…
    7 If you don't know the word, *look it up* in the dictionary.

C 1 circled: outward, economic, darned, capital
    underlined: alone, amiss, glad, asleep

   2 *Cosy* and *dry* – change the *y* to an *i* before adding the ending, e.g. *cosier.* *Flat* and *dim* – double the middle consonant, e.g., *flatter.* *Far* becomes *farther, farthest,* or *further, furthest.* *Good* becomes *better, best.* *Bad* becomes *worse, worst.*

3a of   e for
 b of   f to
 c for   g of
 d with h of

4 (circled words): early, fast, far, right, long

5

Adjectives and adverbs used to talk about:

people	strong 1	decent 2	demanding 2	eccentric	demonstrative
sounds	deep 4	shrill	high 8		
colors	deep 5	delicate 2	bright 2	pastel	
flavors and food	delicate 2	strong 5	bland 1	hot 2	
jobs	demanding 1				
objects, things and materials	strong 2	elastic 1	high 1		

D 1a I don't have *my* own car.
   b He came to Chicago to look for work.
   c The police said there was not enough *evidence* to convict the man.
   d You need permission to park here.
   e I don't have enough *room* for all my books on my shelf.
   f She had the *opportunity* to do an exchange with a student in Italy, *or* She *could* do an exchange with a student in Italy.
   g The thieves broke in and *stole* the TV and the computer.
   h My grandmother can't come to visit me – the long *trip/journey* would be too tiring for her.
   i The family *moved* here three years ago
   j It's *certain* that she'll get a good grade.
   k He used to work for our company, but I don't know where he works *currently.*
   l It's *too big a job* for me to do on my own.

E 1 1 – A 3 – G 5 – C 7 – I 9 – H
    2 – B 4 – F 6 – D 8 – E 10 – J

  2 phat – excellent
    scuzzy – dirty and unpleasant
    wacko – crazy
    wig out – become very excited
    upchuck – vomit
    wack – very bad
    prez – president
    skanky – very unpleasant
    out the wazoo – in large numbers or amounts
    putz around – mess around

7 Pronouncing and spelling words

A 1a • b 4 c No
  2a '
   b ,
  3a vowels and consonants
   b 21 vowel sounds, 26 consonant sounds

B 2b

	ɪ	aɪ	i	æ	ɜ	u	ʌ	e	ɑ
st	*sit*	*sight*	*seat*	*sat*	*set*	*suit*			
ht	*hit*	*height*	*heat*	*hat*		*hoot*	*hut*	*hate*	*hot*
dn	*din*	*dine*	*dean*		*den*				
fl	*fill*	*file*	*feel*		*fell*	*fool*		*fail*	

3 (circled pairs) a, b, e, g, h, i, k, l, n, o, r

4a l 1 c 2 e 1 g 2 i 2
  b 2 d 1 f 2 h 1 j 2

5a W, S b W, S c W, S

6 left – /lɛft/
lift – /lɪft/
leave – /liv/
love – /lʌv/
laugh – /læf/
loaf – /loʊf/
life – /laɪf/

C 1a, c (cos)/tume
or/ni/(thol)/o/gist
ef/(fect)/ive
in/con/(sid)/er/ate
he/(red)/i/ty

2

Nouns	Verbs	Same stress?
pr**o**duce	prod**u**ce	
review	review	✓
object	obj**e**ct	
increase	incr**e**ase	
permit	perm**i**t	
disguise	disguise	✓
desert	des**e**rt	
promise	promise	✓
conduct	cond**u**ct	
cover	cover	✓
conflict	confl**i**ct	

D 1

though
ago toe tow

through
flew tattoo glue

enough
gruff cuff

cough
off

2 a unable e gear
b knock f shoe
c cheese g who
d upset

3a /rʌf/ = rough
/ˈdʒɪŋgl/ = jingle
/ˈklaɪmət/ = climate
/eɪk/ = ache
/ˈkʌstəm/ = custom
/ˈremboʊ/ = rainbow
/zu/ = zoo
/ˈfɑrməsɪst/ = pharmacist

/branz/ = bronze
/loʊ/ = low
/ˈhæbət/ = habit
/ˈskɔrbɔrd/ = scoreboard
/tʃeɪs/ = chase
/saɪz/ = size
/krʌntʃ/ = crunch
/dun/ = dune

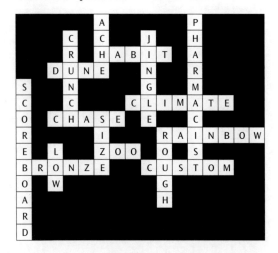

TOPIC 1 Television

1a talk show   e infomercial
b soap opera   f game show
c sitcom   g cartoon
d documentary

2 MARIA: Top 10 Hits; High School, USA; Prom Night Dreams
RALPH: Firearms in our Schools; Law Enforcement Update; Cops on the Beat; Prison Guard
FRANCES: Antique Collecting; Cooking in Grandma's Kitchen; Social Security and Medicare; Your Rights

3a broadcast, satellite   e what's on
b turn off   f channel
c couch potato   g cable TV
d turn up, remote control   h commercial

TOPIC 2 Sports

1 played outdoors: *volleyball, tennis, football, soccer, skiing, ice skating, windsurfing, snowboarding, basketball, hockey, baseball, golf, softball, swimming, jogging, skateboarding*

played with a ball: *volleyball, tennis, football, soccer, table tennis, basketball, baseball, golf, softball, hockey*

played with a racket, paddle or bat: *tennis, table tennis, baseball, softball*

played indoors: *volleyball, tennis, table tennis, ice skating, basketball, hockey, gymnastics, swimming, weightlifting, aerobics*

played on a team: *volleyball, football, soccer, basketball, hockey, baseball, softball*

played with a net: *volleyball, tennis, table tennis, basketball*

played in cold weather: *skiing, ice skating, snowboarding, hockey*

played in water: *windsurfing, swimming*

2a umpire   f match
b court   g coach
c stadium   h field
d referee   i rink
e spectators   j tournament

3a club b stick c bat d racket

TOPIC 3 Shapes

1 (clockwise from top left): square, circle, star, oval, rectangle, crescent, triangle, diamond

2 circle – round or circular
triangle – triangular
rectangle – rectangular
square – square
oval – oval

3 a postcard – rectangular
an egg – oval
your dictionary – rectangular
dice – square
a dinner plate – circular or round
your eyes – oval
a floppy disk – square

4a

noun	adjectives	
		opposite
length	long	short
breadth	broad	narrow
depth	deep	shallow
height	tall/high	short

b a tall woman
   a high brick wall
   a high mountain
   a tall pine tree

5a tall   b deep   c high   d wide

TOPIC 4   Cooking

1
A
a broil   d slice   g roast
b chop   e peel   h fry
c blend   f boil   i defrost
B
blend, boil, chop, peel, roast, slice
C
a peel   b slice   c roast   d boil   e blend   f chop
2
a preheat   d stir   g cool
b soften   e drop   h remove
c mix   f bake   i store

TOPIC 5   Food and shopping

1   3 bags of potato chips
    4 bottles of water
    1 box of chocolates
    1 jar of jam
    1 tube of toothpaste
    6 cans of cola
    1 carton of milk

2   Fred: bacon, fried chicken, ice cream, potato chips
    Amy: ice cream, low-fat yogurt, skim milk, caffè latte
    Sam: bacon, fish, fried chicken

3   curry – India   egg roll – China
    lasagna – Italy   couscous – Africa
    tortilla – Mexico   sangria – Spain
    sushi – Japan   ciabatta – Italy
    pumpernickel – Germany   quesadilla – Mexico
    dim sum – China

4   a a convenience store   e a storeroom
    b a drugstore   f a sweatshop
    c to shoplift   g a shopping cart
    d a workshop

TOPIC 6   Clothes

1   Jill: polka-dotted, patterned
    Liz: flowered, plaid
    Marvin: checked, striped

2   Tom's sweater is not big enough. Kevin's sweater is too big.

3   1 socks   5 pants
    2 sweatshirt 6 pocket
    3 sleeve   7 earmuffs
    4 scarf   Mystery word: sweater

TOPIC 7   Apartment hunting

1a landlord   d superintendent
   b tenant   e deposit
   c rent   f roommate

2   living room: armchair, bookcase, coffee table, couch
    kitchen: dishwasher, refrigerator, sink, stove
    bedroom: bed, bookcase, dresser, mattress
    bathroom: bathtub, shower, sink, toilet

TOPIC 8   Health and fitness

1   Answers on page A32

2a   HMO
 b   health insurance
 c   emergency room
 d   nurse
 e   surgery
 f   clinic
 g   patient
 h   orthodontist

3   ar<u>th</u>ritis, bron<u>ch</u>itis, <u>ch</u>icken pox, <u>ch</u>olera, diar<u>rh</u>ea, laryn<u>g</u>itis,
    leu<u>k</u>emia, <u>mea</u>sles, schizo<u>phr</u>enia, tonsil<u>l</u>itis, <u>wh</u>ooping cough

5   chicken pox, measles
    laryngitis, tonsillitis
    bronchitis, whooping cough
    cholera, diarrhea

TOPIC 9   Business

1 a – 2   c – 10   e – 4   g – 8   i – 7
   b – 3   d – 5   f – 9   h – 1   j – 6

2   Answers will vary.

TOPIC 11   The family tree

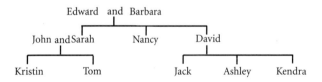

1a   They are cousins
 b   Barbara is John's mother-in-law/John is Barbara's son-in-law
 c   Sarah is Kendra's aunt/Kendra is Sarah's niece

2a   descendant   c ancestor   e single parent
 b   generation   d next of kin   f only child

TOPIC 12   Driving and vehicles

(1) a   (2) b   (3) a   (4) a   (5) b   (6) a
2
a roadkill   c gas station e turn signal g seat belt i steer
b driver's license d headlights   f trunk   h honk   j speeding

TOPIC 13 Tools

1a screwdriver b hammer c drill d pliers e chisel f saw g wrench

2a wrench b saw c chisel d hammer e pliers f screwdriver g drill

3 cutting: chop, rip, slice, tear
fastening: attach, staple, stick, glue

TOPIC 14 Holidays and celebrations

January *New Year's Day*	February *Groundhog Day*	March *St Patrick's Day*
April *April Fool's day*	May	June *Father's Day*
July *Independence Day*	August	September *Labor Day*
October *Halloween*	November *Veterans Day* *Thanksgiving*	December *Christmas* *Kwanzaa*

2 a eggs b practical jokes c hearts d pumpkin pie e Jack-o'-lanterns

3 (clockwise, from top left): the death of a friend's parent, a friend's birthday, Valentine's Day, your parents' anniversary, a baby shower, a friend is in the hospital, Christmas, a friend's graduation from college.

TOPIC 15 The weather

1

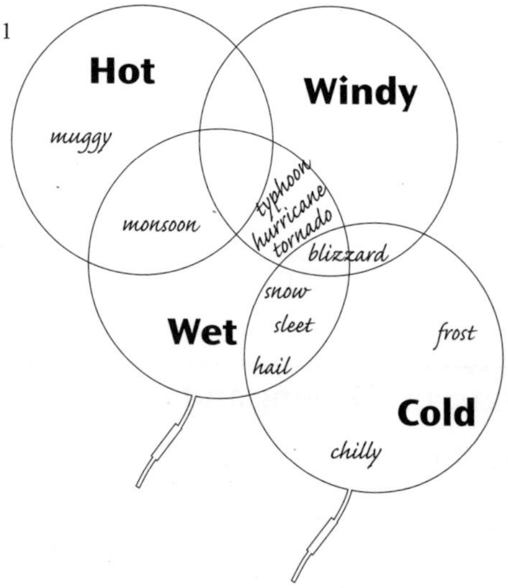

2 a hard b dense c boiling d hard e strong

TOPIC 16 Animals

1 Answers in dictionary.

2

has a long tail	has fur	has sharp teeth	doesn't have any legs	lives in or near water
alligator	beaver	alligator		alligator
beaver	chimpanzee	beaver	worm	beaver
squirrel	squirrel	shark	shark	flamingo
				octopus
				shark

3 sheep – baa
bee – buzz
bird – chirp
cat – meow
cow – moo
horse – neigh
duck – quack
lion – roar

4 dragonfly
armadillo
tarantula
lizard
donkey
skunk
kangaroo

TOPIC 17 Work

1 actor
firefighter
nanny
podiatrist
teacher
electrician
garbage man
midwife
programmer
waiter
engineer
journalist
miner
psychiatrist
farmer
librarian
politician
surgeon

2 1 – g 2 – h 3 – f 4 – d 5 – e 6 – a 7 – b 8 – c

TOPIC 18 Crime and the law

2 plead – guilty or not guilty – **the defendant**
cross-examine – witnesses – **the judge**
return – verdict – **the jury**
pass – sentence – **the judge**
acquit or convict – defendant – **the jury**

3 1 The defendant pleads guilty or not guilty.
2 The judge cross-examines the witnesses.
3 The jury acquits or convicts the defendant.
4 The jury returns a verdict.
5 The judge passes sentence.

4 arraign, guilty, indictment, subpoena, writ

TOPIC 19 Computers

1 screen, mouse, monitor, pointer, keyboard, DVD-ROM drive

2 attachment - e, dialog box - a, double-click - d, IMHO - b, Webcam™ - c

3 1 Web
2 Internet café
3 computer-literate
4 e-zine
5 downloaded
6 hyperlink
7 dotcom
8 e-business
9 DVD
10 ISP
11 surfing
12 information superhighway
13 bookmarking
14 URLs
15 sites
16 favorites
17 e-mail
18 bounce
19 emoticon